THE LIFE AND DEATH
OF PSYCHOANALYSIS

THE LIFE AND DEATH OF PSYCHOANALYSIS

On Unconscious Desire and its Sublimation

Jamieson Webster

Routledge
Taylor & Francis Group

LONDON AND NEW YORK

First published 2011 by
Karnac Books Ltd.

Published 2018 by Routledge
2 Park Square, Milton Park, Abingdon, Oxon OX14 4RN
711 Third Avenue, New York, NY 10017, USA

Routledge is an imprint of the Taylor & Francis Group, an informa business

British Library Cataloguing in Publication Data

A C.I.P. for this book is available from the British Library

ISBN-13: 9781855758995 (pbk)

Typeset by Vikatan Publishing Solutions (P) Ltd., Chennai, India

CONTENTS

For Simon and Soren

ACKNOWLEDGEMENTS

I'd like to thank my colleagues, Lisabeth During, Patricia Gherovici, Ben Kafka, Danny Kaiser, Todd Kesselman, Renata Salecl, and Marc Strauss, for a generous and lasting intellectual friendship. Danny Kaiser deserves credit for introducing me to Adorno over a decade ago. If he hadn't also demonstrated the power of language in Shakespeare, Melville, and Joyce, I might have stayed an Adornian. As well, my gratitude to the inimitable Judith Butler.

I'd like to thank my fellow psychoanalysts without whom I couldn't balance the work of writing about analysis in the midst of practicing it: Nuar Alsadir, Howard Bliwise, Inga Blom, Will Braun, Rachel Gorman, Tehela Nimroody, Vanessa Sinclair; and Helen Zimmer for watching over all of us. A special thanks to Michael Garfinkle, whose commitment as a psychoanalyst has been a continued point of light during the darkest moments of training.

To Norbert Freedman—I will always hear you saying "hello kiddo"— your work on symbolization has provided a much needed bridge between American and French psychoanalysis. I'd like to thank my senior colleagues at the New York Psychoanalytic Institute: Francis Baudry, John Crow, Leon Hoffman, Donald Marcuse, Wendy Olesker, and Herb Wyman.

The dedication of my original dissertation committee deserves recognition: Elliot Jurist, David Lichtenstein, Angelica Nuzzo, Jean-Michel Rabaté, and Lissa Weinstein. I'd like to thank Lissa for offering me freedom with the humility fitting the best of psychoanalysts and supervisors, and Jean-Michel for his rigor, which has helped me think through the problems and merits of my work. I'd like to express an almost inexpressible indebtedness to David Lichtenstein whose grace as a psychoanalyst has been intrinsic to finding anything of my own. That he knows this and I need not say it is one part of what makes this debt so invaluable, like the rare gift of silence from a psychoanalyst.

Last but most—my love and gratitude to my family for enduring with me through this book, especially my son Soren whose patience with me I have been in awe of since the day he was born. To my husband, Simon Critchley—how strange it is to think about the turn my life made all those years ago when you asked Alain "What's up with the math, dude?" in homage to a little conversation between us. This book is inseparable from an encounter with you, with the deepest admiration for the courage of your work and unrelenting passion. I hope that it lives up to you, to what you have given to me. Thank you for making intellectual life such a seamless part of the psychopathology of our everyday life together.

ABOUT THE AUTHOR

Jamieson Webster, PhD, is a psychoanalyst in New York City. She teaches at Eugene Lang College and New York University. Her work focuses on clinical and theoretical psychoanalysis with an interdisciplinary focus on feminine sexuality, philosophy, and aesthetics. This is her first book.

PREFACE

It has been said that this book is something closer to a memoir than a work of scholarship. I don't quite understand the distinction, or rather, I'm not sure what the pressure is on the side of the reader that makes that distinction an important means of orienting oneself in the face of the question—what is this that I have before me? I suppose, in a way, being somewhat without that particular anxiety, I allow myself to blur the line between what is personal and impersonal throughout this work, but it must be said that in doing so, I take Freud as my model.

As Jacques Derrida asked in *To Speculate—On "Freud"* (1991), "how can an autobiographical writing, in the abyss of an unterminated self-analysis, give to a world-wide institution *its* birth?" (p. 531). Perhaps this question, this doubt even, could be transformed into a point of affirmation. It did. Isn't it marvelous? No other institution is born of this same abyss and no other institution must wrestle with it so much as psychoanalysis. Freud is the unmoved mover. Psychoanalysis is one of the strangest but perhaps most astonishing of institutions and practices.

So my anxiety in this work is less about the problems of self-revelation, nor the constraints of autobiography, but rather the life and death of psychoanalysis itself. It is simply a fact that Freud's writing created a worldwide institution. It is perhaps also a fact that this psychoanalytic institution is now in trouble. This historical juncture, over a century after its strange birth, is certainly my point of anxious orientation. While this work begins with the feeling that something of the nature of what is personal and passionate about psychoanalysis has been lost—in particular from the position of a once analysand, now psychoanalyst—rather than expound upon the idea of what has gone missing, which I do not think would take us very far, this work attempts to tell a part of the story of how one becomes a psychoanalyst.

This story cannot be told without saying something about my relationship to psychoanalytic theory and philosophy—that is my training—but intends to use this dialog to show what in psychoanalysis changes the relationship between a subject and thinking, a change in the relationship we hold to knowledge on the whole. This also entails a shift in the love one maintains for precious interlocutors. In fact, I might wager that the former is only possible by virtue of the latter.

Divisions like the one proposed to exist between scholarship and memoir currently exist uncritically in psychoanalysis to a fault, in particular those drawn between theory and practice, or even between truth and falsity, as if memoir, for example, fell easily on one side or the other. I do not abide by this divide, and certainly not as one that is simply so, mapped with any ease. That being said, the incongruous hope of this piece of work is to force these two to work in tandem, and to do so through telling some part of the story of a psychoanalyst's relation to theory in the process of trying to come to terms with what it means to practice psychoanalysis.

Lacan, for one, was often wary of certain false divisions, especially when they obscured a particular set of boundaries crucial to him and to psychoanalytic work; namely, the division between conscious and unconscious, between speaker and spoken of, between body and word, along with the enigma of the difference between the sexes. For Lacan, psychoanalysis uniquely forces a confrontation with these *impossible,* inevitable, divisions and barriers. He noticed that what a patient will come to say to an analyst that will have a critical effect on his or her life will be born as if from this gulf, this abyss.

Significant events seem to gather around these fault lines and highlight them, beyond all conscious intentionality, questioning most claims of ownership. The notion, dare I say hubris, that any given person would be able to sufficiently map a fault of this kind *a priori* is impossible.

Such is the strange impossibility of psychoanalytic work. It is to these divisions and their unique personal elaboration that I am more wed than any contemporary means of orienting a readership.

So with this mind, and by way of an introduction to the work, I'd like to begin with a story that I have come to see as having an important structural relationship to what it was that I wanted to write in this book. In a conversation with the philosopher Alain Badiou, someone who we will spend some time with in this book, the joke of the three second Lacanian session came up: You walk in, barely utter three words, the analyst stands up, the session is finished. It is always one way of dismissing a Lacanian, to bring up an exaggerated version of the practice of cutting a session. Lacanian or not, the psychoanalyst in fantasy, and perhaps in humor as well, is always someone who either throws you out or keeps you forever. And certainly for some, it is difficult to tell whether it is in staying or leaving that one lives or dies.

The joke however, this time around, was meant a little differently. Badiou said that what he would like is to write a philosophical book equivalent to the Lacanian session. Being, Subject, Truth—finished. That was it. Done. This was all that was left for him to say. The sentiment for me in the face of this joke was not only laughter, but also lament. I wish that the joke were true. I wish that was all that needed to be said. I wish that the three-second session worked. Like jokes that play with the impossible, it is funny because we all share the impossible desire to be said and done. It is, in its way, a desire for death—interminable work finding its quickened end.

Badiou has spent far more than three seconds, a lifetime in fact, writing about these words. Perhaps the reason this joke struck me as it did was because his work does in fact cut in the Lacanian sense of cutting through—carving a new edge, creating a new surface. I found in Badiou's work a theoretical clarity and it was a relief to see someone contemporary put psychoanalytic thought to such rigorous use. Badiou, through Lacan, distills the contemporary problems of thought in relation to philosophy, touching on everything from science and mathematics, to art, literature, and politics.

It would not have escaped me that even he, an idealized master who has found a way to cut, longs for an end. The joke, no less the wish— bound by this figure of death—is certainly the dilemma. And it is this dilemma that Badiou uses throughout to frame his theoretical system: the problem, as he calls it, of modernity. To my consternation, it was not from having escaped this dilemma that Badiou recognized it, which would simply be another fantasy that he who leaves is the one who knows. "Modernity," Badiou says,

> means not being able to choose reasonably in what concerns the relation between mastery and truth. Is truth disjoined from the master? .... But then it is entirely obscure .... Is truth conjoined to the master? But in this case, it becomes a sort of immanent terror, an implacable erotic transference ... whether the master is sacrificed to an anonymous power or whether it demands we sacrifice our-selves for the love of him, it is the possibility of choice that vanishes (Badiou, 1998/2005b, p. 53).

Leaving this idealized figure or remaining bound to them is neither a choice. If the possibility of choice vanishes, what else is there to ask for than an end? Eternal categories, such as Being, Subject, and Truth, seem necessary once again. We must, Badiou pleads, find a way to think.

Despite a rich and hardly negligible history between Freudian thought and philosophy, the tie is an increasingly tenuous one. The problems of choice and subjectivity, certainly philosophical problems, were taken up in psychoanalytic theory by Freud in questions concerning love and desire, object-choice, the super-ego, and sublimation, to name just a few. Ironically, if Badiou brings these categories back to the table through a reading of Lacan, he does so quite without the psychoanalytic com-munity. This book tries to lay the ground for a *rapprochement* between psychoanalysis and philosophy—a task much too large for what I wish could be the beauty of a short session.

Nevertheless, these categories, as Badiou named them—Being, Sub-ject, and Truth—have their place in this work. It was in thinking about this joke that I found an important relationship between these catego-ries and the dreams that I had decided to let act as the major organizing force of this work. The dreams seem to contain the joke's very structure. Why these dreams? They are the closest I have gotten to anything like a cutting word, and, it is in their trajectory that I was able to find some means of conclusion. It was through them that I was able to approach this question of the life and death of psychoanalysis, therefore marking the trajectory of a certain path one takes in becoming a psychoanalyst.

This book addresses philosophy and psychoanalysis through the strange medium of my dreams. Psychoanalytically, dreams are, as Freud perhaps too famously said, the royal road, and being a psychoanalyst it is the only road I know how to take. Is this really the place to cross once again with this much older discipline? You'll have to decide for yourself. Dreams, as we know, formally condense an almost infinite number of threads into an image, narrative, or sensation, in something not unlike the span of seconds, often with a biting sense of humor or punning. This determination provided me with a certain momentum that felt necessary and intrinsic to this work, a movement that went from theory to dream, and from dream back to theory.

Psychoanalytically speaking, this does not mean that the work or dream is closed-in, and just as the cutting short of a session brings it to an end, however quickly, it is also meant to provide or provoke the place of an opening. So it was in the process of writing about these dreams that I realized that they had some equivalence to what was a passing joke between someone I greatly admire and myself. Sometimes jokes can be the best of all possible interpretations.

This work revolves around three dreams and three figures. The first dream that you will read, *the vase and the letter*, situates a question using the image from the dream of a letter sealed inside the hollow of a vase. The letter comes to represent the attempt to secure an identity, most intimately that of being a psychoanalyst, beyond or before the constraints of the vacuity of that position—its impossible authorization. It is close to Badiou's definition of Being as void found in this image of the vase as a construction around an interior emptiness. Badiou's definition of Being comes close to the important place that the body holds in psychoanalysis, the body acting as a negative center for the subject with the importance of the *letter* of language that defines the cutting edge between a body and a subject. Speech is only a possible horizon thereafter.

Badiou's magnum opus, *Being and Event* (1988/2005a), positions the classical philosophical question of ontology—the question of Being, of that which is—against what can never be accounted for by its ground, namely, the unforeseen or unforseeable event. It is Badiou's way, to put it somewhat crudely, of reinterpreting the poles of objectivity and subjectivity, empirical ground and an ephemeral happening always subject to interpretation.

For Badiou, ontology is a concept that must be formalized. In particular, Badiou seeks to formalize the question of Being through a mathematical notion of absence or the void, close to the concept of a set in set theory mathematics. Being is a necessary point of emptiness without which we could not account for our system of thought. In the first dream, that point of emptiness, represented by the hollow of the vase, becomes critical to any understanding of the wish to be a psychoanalyst. To be an analyst is to endure a fundamental relation to absence and loss.

The second dream, *the memorial of impossibility*, addresses a certain problem concerning the Subject. The dream's desperation, what comes to be represented by a memorial of the events of September 11th, is the desperation of a desire for a subjectivity that feels firm, even if that means, as it so often does, holding on to infirmity and trauma itself. Subjectivity can become a point of endless lament and just as the difficulties of life are easily transformed into melancholia, truth does not necessarily become a foundation for affirmation. Badiou's work, perhaps above all else, is always directed towards the hope of this affirmation of the subject.

The subject for Badiou is something like an event that marks a constitutive break from the multiplicity or general heterogeneity of life, like a distinct sound emerging from a field of noise, or, perhaps better, like one purpose of erecting a memorial as a way to mark the importance of a day in an infinite span of time. The Subject is rare and precarious in its mode of appearance, and in that sense, close to Lacan's concept of the subject as a subject of the unconscious.

The subject is not something that is merely given; it is not granted *a priori*. Another definition of the subject that might be fitting, if not controversial, would be the subject as continually constructed and reconstructed—this process having its relevance for both the image of the fallen towers and trauma itself. Of course for Lacan, the subject is always the subject of speech, who, rather than being the one that carries on in the blah, blah of day-to-day chatter, is instead the one opened out by the listening analyst and the unconscious determinants marked by that ear.

Memorials, far from existing in this place of radical opening, are more often than not a means of attachment to some past impossibility. The two interpretations are at odds in this dream. In actuality the first dream in this book (*the vase and the letter*) was dreamt second, and the actual first dream (*the memorial*) was partially misinterpreted by me in line with this cruelty of melancholia—particularly during the many years of analytic work that constitutes the space between the two dreams. It was an important misinterpretation, demonstrating something of the difficulty of situating a subject in relation to their unconscious desire. The refusal of any opening, a subjectivity that falters in and through misinterpretation and the wish propelling it, finds a means of reversal by virtue of what the second dream is able to mark. Perhaps one must think the void, construct the place of a certain kind of emptiness or absence, before being able to locate and take hold of this elusive subject—impossible without desire.

The retroactive force of meaning, what Freud called *nachträglichkeit*, is the impetus behind reversing their presentation to you. There have to be two times, two events, for Freud, whose retroactive effects he reads. This structure cuts through the past via a repetition introduced by the backward trajectory. The past only makes sense in reference to the future and the future anterior is the grammatical tense of desire whose essence is this moebius-like structure. Against what many assume is a fascination with digging up the past, here, we are clearing the way forward.

For Badiou, the redefinition of these concepts—Being, Subject, and Truth—under the influence of Lacan, also meant a way forward. It meant for him that philosophy could finally, hopefully, confront the problem of nihilism. A tension between nihilism and desire is certainly one problem staged in the space between these two dreams. As you will come to see, these dreams have a critical effect on my reading of philosophy, and in particular of those philosophers working in the aftermath of World War II, a time that certainly confounds the problems of negativity and the subject with a terror of annihilation.

So the dream of *the vase and the letter* allowed me to rethink the first dream, a process which changed not only my understanding of the memorial, but my memory of that time in analysis as well. It is in the third dream, the dream of *A Book Called Instructions On How To Fell A Tree*, after this movement back and forth, open and closed, through progress and failure, that I was able to imagine the possibility of psychoanalysis. The desire of the analyst to be a psychoanalyst was not there before, only after. This, it seems crucial to note, was the last dream to take place within the time that I was in analysis.

The work with these dreams speaks to the important place of unconscious desire. Dream objects that are also *dreams of objects* give a kind of pure formality to this unfolding elaboration. It is my hope that these dreams have something to say about these age-old philosophical categories, in particular, the critical relationship between a subject and his or her objects. The impossible tie between a subject and an object, a source of irrefutable splitting, cannot, from the perspective of psychoanalysis, be elaborated without getting closer to unconscious desire. I have taken the chance of doing so through the elaboration of these dreams.

It is time I said something about unconscious desire, perhaps the central category of this work. Unconscious desire, as the Lacanians have understood it—taking their departure from the idea of wish in the *Interpretation of Dreams*—is what creates the combinatory formula that structures the dream, or the joke as the case may be, which is always more *formal* than meaningful. Dreams were to take us to the very limits of the human, and, in a way, what is discovered is that desire is equivalent to this act: desire is a desire for transgression. What this means for Lacan is that desire cannot be reduced to the object, nor can it be entirely reduced to the subject either, holding a dimension in its own right that begins to define the space and organization of the unconscious. In this, it is closely bound to the Freudian drive.

Desire is not only that which pushes the limits of self or others—an interpretation that I think has unfairly given desire a fearsome Hobbesian character—but also that which is able to intimately trace these limits and how we've constructed and defined them for ourselves. The latter definition, for my purposes, is the more interesting no less more generous one. The search becomes intrinsic to the definition of desire both literally and figuratively, informing the aim of psychoanalysis.

Desire, for Lacan, cannot be separated from its appearance in language and images, in dreams and daydreams, in jokes and slips of the tongue, and of course in symptoms. Always short of the final transgression it seeks, desire is bound to its own means of representation. Symbolizing, to my ear, always bears this impossible movement of desire in an inimitable formal consistency. Without this structure, even without this inherent formalism, I don't think it would be possible to create a dream. The portion of it that is unconscious, and no doubt will remain so, touches on the most obscure and formative aspects of the human psyche from archaic memories to infantile fantasies.

It is for this reason that I have chosen to structure this work based on the series of dreams coupled with transferences to important figures. I do so with the hope that this provokes the kind of reading of desire that will touch on its most elusive formal mechanisms. The concern with the life and death of psychoanalysis comes from a feeling that this way of understanding desire, this way of working with it, indeed at times even glorifying it, has been lost. Even further that the felt danger of working at such an extreme limit, which is the very limit of the *human*, is the fascinating difficulty that sustains the psychoanalytic act. At times it feels that we have forgotten the value of this kind of reading of desire, and even more so, the difficulty, the time-consuming and careful work of locating it in an analysis.

Serge Leclaire, in his book *Psychoanalyzing* (1968/1998b), has an astonishing reading of Freud's desire through careful attention to the imagery, language, and the formal mechanisms, inherent in Freud's dreams (1900). He uses the essay on screen memories (1899) which we know to be autobiographical, along with the biographical material of Freud's life that follows his self-analysis (1985)—particularly that which comes to the fore in the letters with Fliess. Leclaire, going back over the early Freud, charts out the subtleties of Freud's desire using its linguistic and what he calls phantasmatic or Oedipal components.

Leclaire notes the closeness of the word loaf in his screen memory to the word body in German, acoustically indistinguishable (*Laib*, *Leib*); Freud biting (*beissen*) into the loaf of bread shortly after snatching (*entre-issen*) flowers from his little cousin Pauline; and the people with bird's beaks (bird, *Vogel*, is too close to *vögeln*, a vulgar word for the sexual act, to ignore) that carry his mother in a dream, her face the image of both death and beatitude, whose cause, he says, Freud no doubt imagines himself to be. It is, he says, the mother who smiles or fails to smile on her hero son. He follows the centrality of the *botanical* book torn or ripped (*reissen*) to shreds at the bidding of his father, like the flowers he ripped from his first love's hands, Pauline, or, the devouring of his favorite flower the artichoke.

All of this, Leclaire contends, seems to culminate in a desire to write the book on the secret of dreams precisely as a fulfillment of it. Freud's book of dreams folds in on itself: a book about dreams of writing the book about dreams. Leclaire finds circulating again and again the formula of Freud's desire—to reveal, unveil, plumb, rip, tear, bite, pick, pluck. It is not such a far leap to Freud's one major symptom, from the wish to tear into and reveal to his phobia of travel (from *reissen* to *reisen*), where indeed the incestuous link can be found when as a young child Freud glimpsed his mother nude on a journey (also *Reisen*).

Leclaire says, "at this point in the analysis, we can already see the outline of the profoundly intricate relation between book and woman, leaf and flower picking, picking (flowers) and eating … the way in which Sigmund relates this (screen) memory seems indeed to indicate what he made of this singular form of "reading": an extraordinarily satisfying defoliation and transgression" (pp. 26–27). If Freud wanted to tear or rip the veil off the secret of dreams, the phantasmatic portion of that desire—by which I mean the impossible image of its Oedipal satisfaction, notably in an act of ripping into or devouring the object—suggests that we cannot follow Freud there. This end fulfillment of desire can only be death itself; oral incorporation wrapped in the nature of the phantasm. The discovery of unconscious desire, for Leclaire, is not synonymous with the image of satisfaction that one's fantasy proffers.

When investigating the repression of an accident at a young age that left a scar on his jaw, Freud himself points to an intensity of fury and guilt around the birth of his brother Julius who died about the time of this accident. Leclaire feels this to be close to the consequences of the Oedipal phantasm: Freud's "greediness that knew no obstacles," in relation to his mother, against his brother, books, and cigars. The last, cigars, would return him to the scene of this original scar and be his final undoing. As he would write to Fliess, "moderation is the hardest thing for the child, as for the neurotic" (Freud, 1985, p. 365).

Unconscious desire is more closely allied to its formal mechanisms—from primary process to the logic of unconscious fantasy—which must be distinct from the content that these manipulate. What Freud reveals to us then is the secret of dreams *as* unconscious desire which, taken in itself, is not necessarily equivalent to revealing as in lying open like a book to be torn to shreds—what Leclaire calls the substitute that Freud's father offered to Freud for his Oedipal phantasm. We know the difficulty with books Freud got into in his adolescence. What Leclaire emphasizes is that there is desire and there is the object that causes desire. Psychoanalysis centers itself on the importance of this asymmetry or divide. These memories of Freud's are only a screen that betrays the wish, and the wish is but a cipher for a constantly renewed construction.

For Leclaire, as Lacan, desire is bound to the lack from which it springs—not having one's mother as the object of haste. Leclaire will say that what psychoanalysis teaches us is that desire in this purest formal sense is a desire for transgression, a desire for a movement that goes beyond, but which cannot. So one must pass through the castration complex, encountering a desire that cannot completely accommodate itself to the object that seems to hold it captive. It is from this constellation that Leclaire iterates a series of consequences for psychoanalysis based on this reading of desire with Freud's. I take these consequences as my own throughout this work and innumerate them here at the outset:

> To grasp what psychoanalysis imposes on us, then, as Freud never
> tires of saying, we still have to get rid of many prejudices. And

especially here we must rid ourselves of two major habits: first, the way of considering the tension of desire on the model of the appeal to a need turned expectantly in the direction of an object that would be the proper one to gratify it. Obviously, psychoanalysis proposes no such thing, for *unconscious desire appears there as a formula*, surprising in its oddity, often absurd, a composite like the figure of an Egyptian god … It is a formula, cipher, or letter that aims more at insisting, at repeating itself enigmatically than at saturating, gratifying, or suturing in some fashion.

The other prejudice that psychoanalysis leads us necessarily to renounce is … the notion of the distinction between a deeply hidden and truthful reality, on the one hand, and a deceptive appearance, a directly accessible surface, on the other. To be sure, the didactic opposition between manifest and latent content allows for a limited interpretation, thereby sustaining this prejudice. Yet, notice how in the course of our reading *one and the same term* turns out in fact, upon analysis, to support the truth and its veiling …. We cannot insist too much here on this fact, which is coextensive with the whole possibility of psychoanalysis, namely: *there is no truth either before or beyond unconscious desire; the formula that constitutes it at the same time represents it and betrays it* …

Finally, oddly enough, what appears at the end of an uncompromising analysis is unconscious desire itself as a formal construction and, as such, devoid of meaning but easily couched in a figure … in its phantasmatic composition … in its hieroglyphic concision. We therefore find at the end of the analysis a formal composition analogous to that of the rebus with which we began. But this formal composition also turns out to be the very essence of the latent thoughts that nothing, or almost nothing distinguishes from the manifest content, either in its terms or its organization. There could be no better illustration of the fact, crucial for analysis, that there is nothing beyond the text, or better yet, the letter (Leclaire, 1968/1998b, pp. 36–37).

For Leclaire, there cannot be a meta-discourse in psychoanalytic work. This does not mean that there isn't a value to a psychoanalyst's thinking through certain meta-psychological questions, certainly Leclaire does, but it is precisely in thinking these questions through to their very limits that one is always returned to the letter of the unconscious of which there is, as he says, nothing beyond. This letter is the closest we get to unconscious desire in its pure form, a fact which led Lacan to say something as absurd as *the unconscious is structured like a language*.

Truth, in this mode of appearance, is continuous with its surface manifestations. Not beneath or before it. Desire is equivalent to its constructed form (Leclaire would even say formula or composition). The *meta* in clinical work is prohibited. We no longer abide by a theory of abreaction and one should question the ultimate value of thinking in terms of manifest and latent content. Play at the surface, as we saw in the analysis of Freud, is coextensive with the psychoanalytic work necessary for elaborating on the question of one's desire.

Too often in psychoanalysis desire remains abstract, banalized, or both—as in, he wanted to sleep with his mother, he wanted to kill his father, or worse, he had a sexual urge, he was angry—i.e., fundamentally meaningless statements. We suffer not from desire but from desire's unarticulated specificity. It is desire's absolute specificity that Leclaire sees as the result of an uncompromising psychoanalysis.

Psychoanalysis works by virtue of a respect for this unknown or Other desire which is brought to speech. Freud's offhand comment that one learns to know when to stop interpreting a dream seems to me close to this ethic. In fact, it is in knowing how to stop that we are able to recognize something of the dream's navel, the differently centered center of the dream. For Leclaire, it is this very tact with interpretation that mirrors a working through of the consequences of Oedipus—a confrontation with desire and its limits that is synonymous with its fullest articulation. It is this orientation that gives back to desire its medium, and so hopefully too, its means of moderation.

It should be said that despite the linguistic aspects of Leclaire's reading, the body, affect, are not categories that are ever far off. If these words he maps have any consequence it is because they contain an indissoluble tie to the body, in particular, the body as experienced and imagined by the child Freud. It is these words that seem to retain their contact with this ineffable thing we call a body, hallucinatory intensity always one signifier of this revival. It is only this strange tenuous tie, ever-present in the world of words and dreams, which enables analysts to do their particular work of reading or listening to desire. No one, to my mind, illustrates this better than Leclaire. It is to his definition of psychoanalytic work as a work with the formula or structure of desire, tracing its tie to a phantasmatic object in all its most ardent and bodily particularity, that *this* work is constructed and bound.

Freud's dream of self-dissection and his anxiety about having exposed himself so extensively in his book of dreams is a partially present anxiety for me. I am well aware of the reversing and traversing phallic imagery in my dreams, themes of castration, death, empty cavities, and the like. While this populates my imagination, is at the foundation of the work I do with patients, providing markers in any process of association, I am using these dreams less as reductive, interpretable, indeed dissectible entities, and more as a provocation to thought, which, like the Lacanian cut, may be of use to gain some ground with respect to unconscious desire. Maybe I could have done without them. Less revealing in any case. But, the dream written about is something transformed, close to sublimation, out of a hallucination, which is the very possibility of thought.

If we take this further to include what Leclaire says about the nature of desire—it always supports the truth at the same time as it conceals it—revealing as knowledge is never the truth of desire. It is not an act of full disclosure. "As you know," Freud said, "a beautiful dream and no indiscretion, do not coincide" (Freud, 1985, p. 315). This shifts the difficulty, as I see it, from the problem of my telling a dream to one concerning the reading of it. My hope is for these dreams, rebus-like, to provide some kind of key for a new reading of desire; that these dreams act as a way station beyond the kind of knowledge whose stasis is contrary to the intended object of this work. In the vein of what the Christian mystical philosopher Simone Weil says in *Gravity and Grace*, "it is necessary to touch impossibility in order to come out of the dream world. There is no impossibility in dreams—only impotence" (Weil, 1947/1952, p. 95).

Might these dreams allow us to come out of the dream world? To touch impossibility? To the psychoanalysts, I ask, give me this leisure. To the philosophers, I ask, tolerate a little intimacy. These dreams are bound by intellectual figures that may or may not give you the space you seek in knowing. But I am too acutely aware at most points in time, at all points in writing, that too much distance renders any truth arid and ineffective. So my voice is present. There is a degree of intimacy. But that voice makes its appearance as readily as it disappears under the weight of an academic dialogue—an obsessive undertaking of another's thought.

Do I fail to be scholarly because I cannot quiet my hysterical disappointment? Fail because I cannot divest myself of this underside of discourse? Yes, I would say that I do fail, but that what is scholarly is another matter. For now, all I can do is give myself over to this play and this failure in order to learn once again how to live with psychoanalysis, with *The Life and Death of Psychoanalysis*. To all of my readers, I ask, give me your patience and tolerate a little dislocation. As in love perhaps something will come of it.

CHAPTER ONE

Fatigue and haste

I am tired. Psychoanalysis makes me incredibly tired. I have spent a greater part of my time hating psychoanalysis. I can't read another paper. I want the whole thing to collapse. I see it teetering on the edge of its abyss, and think I'm done, it is done. And yet somehow I know that it could do nothing else—it is precarious, it has been from the beginning. What have I been hoping for? What did I expect? Apparently a whole lot. It is an understatement to say that I am betrayed both by disappointment and this constancy of hope. I have never allowed this the label of pathology. Better yet, I will never allow this. Label implies stasis. So does my never.

I hear the voice of Rapaport (1967), a member of Lacan's enemy camp, cautioning the psychoanalysts that structure is that *only amenable to a very slow rate of change*. Never get ahead of yourself. Know your limits as a psychoanalyst. I want to tell him psychoanalysis is in too much jeopardy for this *slow rate of change*. Never say never then also. Nothing is without its pathos. But I am myself too slow for this structural pathos that catches up on you faster than you can imagine. Hope what you will. Psychoanalysis will remain precarious.

We seem to be doing our best to back away from what has always been this precarious place of psychoanalytic truth. Science isn't going

1

to seal up that hole and remove the abyss. Neither will any recourse to folk psychology or Lacanian mathematical formulas. I'm sure my theories won't seal off this hole either, which is what I am beginning to suspect that I have expected as well. Pathos is quick, like fantasy arising in the place of any disjunction.

So we should not be so hasty. Psychoanalysis from day one circled around this question of *pathos* and structure. What emerges instead of declared ends or hasty beginnings seems to be a question about what it really means to begin or end. "Now we have finally begun," the analyst thinks, not necessarily at the first session, but maybe three months down the line or even longer as the case may be. Before that moment, the work has not constituted this kind of opening, and, as is the case with psychoanalysts, we must wait. We do not know when this time will arrive. In fact, most often we only know it after it has passed, as in the *now we have* which marks the point in passing.

In light of this, let me tell you about a dream I had. I was reaching up into an attic and I found a vase. Inside the vase, in its empty cavity, was a letter sealed into its edge, the internal periphery. The letter turned out to be from my maternal grandmother, sometime in the 1970s from the Philippines seemingly addressed to no-one in particular. This is also to say also that it was written specifically for me. In the letter she states that she has read a book, Laplanche's *Life and Death in Psychoanalysis (1970/1976)*, and that it has not yet been translated but that it would come to be a very important text. This is the scene, now what was the wish?

This undistributed letter granted me the authority as analyst that I am constantly looking for. Here, in the form of a wished for matrilineal inheritance. That was it. There was no ambiguity. It was written in the stars. You were born to do this kind of thing, I remembered being told when I was young. I could be done with myself and with my nagging questions about psychoanalysis. Both are transparent. All was revealed in the secrets of my history. It would come to be very important, as my grandmother said. That was a fact. It would come.

When I am working, trudging along in an analysis, I often wish it would work this way. The curtain goes up, the act is performed, we applaud, and in no short time, the curtain comes down again. We both leave the theater. I think Freud also wanted the work to conclude in such a way. As we said before, his desire to be the ultimate transgressor, to lift the veil, to reveal all, was a point of fantastic closure. In any case, if it did work in such a fashion, I don't think I would be where I am—dreaming of empty cavities, full of imagined histories, and in the end very, very tired.

There is an old psychoanalytic joke about what a woman means when she says she can't cook. It is her reproach against her mother for leaving her with a question concerning her feminine sexuality—for having failed to teach her. As jokes go, it's really not that funny, but it is there in the dream. Hysteria takes the form of a vase and a wished for matrilineal inheritance. One might begin to see that the question of the desire to be an analyst and the desire of the analyst are already at play, in minimal form as something you would like to find inscribed like a letter on your body, something that is painfully connected to questions of femininity.

Psychoanalysis, I might say, rests on a precarious ethics that demands one steer clear of any fantasy of closure. That one can imagine psychoanalytic work as precisely this kind of closure is why we are required to go into it. This difficulty, the tenuousness of any opening, is easily papered over—with meaning first off. Certainly if there is a desire to be an analyst, the consequences of that wish can open out in a psychoanalysis; but this would only be possible if the listening analyst does not feel he or she can provide an answer to this impossible desire. Psychoanalysis from the very beginning cannot but pose a question of what its own teaching or transmission consists of.

I remember my first confrontation with a woman analyst. I was a little older than twenty. I sheepishly told her I wanted to be a psychoanalyst and she replied that I had to understand my desire to be an analyst before anything else and casually ate a banana. I ran away after that meeting. I was only able to approach her again a decade or so later. At first I thought there must be something terrifying about this desire she intuited that I didn't understand or seem to know anything about. A little bit later I think the command *to understand,* more than anything else, was what terrified me. To our desire, we can accommodate ourselves. To others, knowledge, that takes a little more work. I was newly in analysis. I was also new to Lacan.

The dream of the vase was a dream close to the end of my analysis. If what we can locate in psychoanalysis *is* unconscious desire such that it can be taken up as the desire of the analyst, then it would follow that such commandments (in particular *to understand,* as if that had anything to do with desire) should finally have less effect on me—that I couldn't be put on the run. It is for this reason that Lacan (1986/1992) takes up the question of desire in the guise of the courage of Antigone in the face of Creon. His laws were bound to a form of closure and authority. She was, in her way, true to a desire beyond his Law.

In this same seminar, *The Ethics of Psychoanalysis 1959–1960*, Lacan also speaks about a vase. He plays with Heidegger's (Heidegger, 1971) notion of the vase as the Thing, or *das Ding*, particularly as it relates to human creation. Creation is like the event-character of Being, Heidegger contends. It is something whose proximity and nearness is veiled, situated between earth and sky, between the terrestrial and celestial, between gods and mortals—what Heidegger calls "the fourfold" (Heidegger, 1993). The vase offers us up to the Heavens at the same time that it is grounded in the earth from which it fashions itself.

This is close to how Lacan defines the signifier in its purest dimension—the emergence of a signifier as signifier, without any proper ground or signified upon which to rest. Human creation for Lacan cannot be understood without reference to the importance of language and symbolism, and furthermore, there is always a dimension of the signifier that signifies something of the act of signification itself. Contained in the signifier is this movement of reaching suspension, from nothing toward something, that is at the essence of the signifier exemplified in the vase:

> If it is really a signifier, and the first of such signifiers fashioned by human hand, it is in its signifying essence a signifier of nothing other than of signifying as such or, in other words, of no particular signified …. Emptiness and fullness are introduced into a world that by its self knows not of them …. And it is exactly in the same sense that speech may be full or empty …. And that is why the potter, just like you to whom I am speaking, creates the vase with his hand around this emptiness, creates it, just like the mythical creator, *ex nihilo*, starting with a hole (Lacan, 1986/1992, pp. 120–122).

This vase is the human object of creation *par excellence*. Wherever we find them, they mark the presence of the human. The human gift of creation is one that brings emptiness into existence, and by virtue of this, the dream of filling it once and for all. Before it, as he says, the world knows not of it. Psychoanalysis gives particular meaning to this

Thing or *nihil* upon which the world is fashioned through desire. The vase establishes a trajectory. The thing, impossible, is both the origin and the aim.

The letter, my letter, comes with this introduction of emptiness—it rests upon it, indeed in the literal image of the dream. This nothing or *nihil* creates the dream of a wished for authority precisely at the point where the question of being a woman and being a psychoanalyst irrevocably cross. The letter remains closed and unopened—unsent. The letter as such seems to try to close in space, asking for something to exist beyond signification, perhaps beyond even address.

There was something about the feeling of reaching; reaching into an attic, only then to have to reach further, into a vase, into the letter. The point of satisfaction was with the letter. It's imagined history acted as a stopping point. Thinking of this, I was reminded that in the houses in which I lived as a child we couldn't build basements. The water table is too high. The idea that the earth wasn't solid, that water was not just all around but below as well seemed to imply that the only direction to reach was upward. That the Philippines consist of thousands upon thousands of islands is another aspect of the felt absurdity in this dream. How did this text get there? How would it have gotten off?

The Philippines, in my memory, was always a terrifying place either without identity or with too much of it—the effects of having had one colonizer after another. Paris in the 1970s, on the other hand, is, for me, the heights of an intellectual movement I have devoted much of my time to. Something here is certainly at play—identity and the ravaging of it, civilized life and something more primal, land and water, reaching upward and the fear of sinking below. Points of identification seem to multiply and unravel in these shifting associations.

Perhaps in light of this we should place in opposition the heights of attics with the basements or earth where these artifacts are usually found. I am reminded of Freud's cautionary note to Binswanger (1957), quoted in the latter's memoir of their friendship:

> I have always confined myself to the ground floor and basement of the edifice—You maintain that by changing one's point of view, one can also see an upper story in which dwell such distinguished guests as religion, art, etc. You are not the only one to say this; most cultured specimens of *homo natura* think the same thing. In this you are conservative, and I revolutionary (pp. 96–97).

Binswanger reaches for sublimation too quickly. Any inheritance, taken as a direct line, will always be conservative. What Freud does in isolating himself on the ground floor is to attempt something more radical than this.

Psychoanalytic work, as it is elaborated in this dream, *is* fatiguing—confined to the basement we cannot reach too quickly for the light. We must work there where the line between dream and reality, between the human world and the inhuman, even between good and evil, is one that comes seriously under question. Weariness, fatigue, cannot be done away with—something solid ground or exalted heights would seem to offer. One must find a way to be permitted to be weary—to let oneself be submerged.

My maternal grandmother, the same one who wrote the letter, used to say to me "Jack of all trades, master of none" because, as the story goes, I would never finish projects before I was on to the next. Maybe I was lucky despite my grandmother's consternation. What frustrates me is a question concerning education, pedagogy—that assumptions must be made that one knows, has something to give, has been given something, performs the outcome of this exchange, and so has made certain progress. This is where the discipline of psychoanalysis generally suffers. Standards of training are always the crisis.

When is one ready to be a psychoanalyst? Who has the authority to decide such a thing? Who declares the analyst done, fit, competent, learned, master? For my part, this process cannot be controlled, however much the ambiguity might seem to force us in this direction toward imagined histories that legitimate. So I feel like I could say to you the main thesis of this work, just as my grandmother said it to me, but I will reverse the negation into an affirmation—Jack of all trades, master of none. And I'm done. I was always hasty. But, if it were simply a matter of stating it, a matter of commandment, positive or negative, then there wouldn't be a need for psychoanalysis.

Freud understood this. He also shares an unfortunate sense of haste. One can marvel at his radical impatience with himself and with Fliess in his letters at the time of his self-analysis: "the time for hypnosis is up ... In all haste, your Dr. Freud" (Freud, 1985, p. 22). His irritation and confusion, particularly when he feels "incapable of mastering it all," loom large in these early letter. He tells Fliess he feels "beaten and disenchanted," "fatigued"—all these wonderful vicissitudes of haste. He concludes this last letter, "I now feel a void."

If Freud's letter expresses his desire to "catch a *Pater* as the originator of neurosis" thereby putting an end to his "ever recurring doubts," it is not the fulfillment of this wish that in fact makes Freud work, or indeed makes his work any good, but a putting to use of the wish. He recognizes something of its impossibility (Freud, 1985, pp. 150–151). This, I would speculate, begins in a working through of his transference relationship to Fliess—his love, his most cordial friend, his tyrant, as he called him. In this, Freud will not back away from a discovery that feels transgressive, as he had done earlier, to his great pain, with the cocaine experiment.

If we are to understand the beginning of psychoanalysis, the faltering way it comes into being through the interpretation of Freud's dreams, we must return to Freud's feeling of failure with respect to Fliess. For a time, he was always ashamed and incommensurate, crystallizing this internal obstacle in the figure of his analyst. Freud's questioning and search for his own authority can be seen in almost every dream—his nightmare of his work as a mausoleum of shit, and the wish for the better cure, Irma's injection. The question of authority paralyzes him.

Through Freud's developing transference to Fliess we can see the elaboration of this paralysis into a terrifying desire to push further. Rome, travel, discovery, and dreams. In the beginning, perhaps you only need one person who listens, or even that you imagine listens, to elaborate on an unknown terror, and, to encounter the field that emanates the orders of inhibition. This situation—imagined protector, imagined persecutor—is ripe. There is one there who seems to be the cause. In the end, that Freud would be able to write on his own, without Fliess, is what we analysts call, with too much triviality, the working through of the castration complex.

Beyond whatever fantasy, it is also Fliess' support of Freud's transference, hinged on very little, that offered to Freud the possibility of taking up his desire. Despite the bad reputation that haunts Fliess, I think you can see in these letters that, more or less, he lets Freud be. This enables Freud to exchange his transference for a flurry of creativity, his depression transforming into enduring enthusiasm. In this way, dreams and reverence are indispensable to this beginning act in order that it may act as a real beginning.

The presence of the letter in the vase holds this very susceptibility to reverence. The command for mastery can be just as much a demand for love. Identification forms a closed circle—from myself to my grandmother and back around again. This circle, in essence, must break. We must find a way for our desire not to be swallowed by our own families. The wished for inheritance is one among many covers for an incestuous tie gratifying for the child who wishes only to be the apple of their mother's eye. The Oedipal prohibition descends with all its ambivalence and unfolding strife. So you would like to leave the Philippines behind? What use do the French have for a girl like you?

This particular Oedipal brand of narcissism, the dilemma between narcissism and desire, acts like a wall Freud keeps accidentally banging his head against; the problem simply won't go away. Indeed, its vicissitudes become for Freud exactly that which we inherit in our advanced state of civilization: discontent or *Unbehagen*. The internalization of the authority of parental figures exists at the far end of this trajectory of identification. Between the ego-ideal and the superego wishes multiply and conflict in the range established by this process. We move from the desire for absolute correspondence to the aggressivity of a conclusive eclipse. I am, after all, the one who is writing the book, *Life and Death*.

Lacan (1970/2006) begins his discourse from this point with his conception of the mirror stage. Narcissism, the dialectic between body and reflexive self-image in the development of the structure of the ego, is something like a necessary failure. For Lacan it is important to understand how easily difference, what is beyond the ego, collapses into a desire for sameness and mastery—at root in any narcissistic structure. To see one's self in the other, like with like, cannot but arouse one's aggression. This aspect of the ego is formed like the successive peels of an onion. At bottom, for Lacan, is always desire. What else initiated the search?

The ego has difficulty with this want-to-be given definition through the precipitation of an ideal image that, far from being a nourishing image, is more often a deadly one whereby we founder in the gap. The possibility of a beyond is always, for Lacan, pointed to more by this *wanting* or desiring than the imagoes themselves. The gap must remain. I am always less than what I, or even they, wanted me to be, but also, I am more the less. The discrepancy is the source, for Lacan, of the life of desire.

Unconscious desire will retain the capacity to cut through the imaginary agglutination of the ego that stagnates at this point of narcissistic capture. Structurally this is also the possibility of another way of thinking about the subject. The subject is closer to this *wanting* than the image itself. Lacan called this subject the subject of the unconscious, the subject as desire of the Other, the subject of the signifier. You may have heard all these Lacanian catch-phrases. But that is precisely the difficulty. If they are something heard-before, something worn down or worn out, they do not proceed by the logic that Lacan is trying to abide by in the sense of an unconscious that is able to surprise or disrupt the expected image.

What Lacan hoped would come from psychoanalytic work with unconscious desire, as well as its theoretical working over, would have to be something beyond a static image or ideal. Our knowledge would have to be something that didn't belabor the problems of narcissism. Knowledge, accumulated in the service of mastery or a unified self-image, is antithetical to our clinical work, so why not also our theoretical work and teaching?

To go back to Freud, he seems to consistently point to the place where something is missing in knowledge that has consequences for a subject. He had funny ways of talking about it beyond the ubiquity of repression—sometimes it was death, accepting the vaginal orifice, the impossible certainty that one's father is one's father, even, interuterine memories and the pulsations of the body and organs. The point was that something escapes that nonetheless has consequences. Or rather, it is that which escapes that holds the greatest consequences.

Working through implies, at least in part, working through an egoistic derision for this errant life of desire. Lacan, in struggling at every step with the virtues and vices of this *something lacking*, tries to mirror this act of working through. I take this to mean that the question of whether or not I, or anyone, is to escape reverence, fatigue, or haste, is not quite what is at stake. The passion, no less impatient frustration of the hysteric, is not the problem. For Lacan, it may even be the solution.

If there was a time when Lacan was writing that many were able to return to Freud with fresh eyes then his theoretical work functioned in the vein of a good interpretation. It is productive. Good interpretations for Lacan have something to do with putting into relief the place of absence, what escapes, which makes room for the passions of a subject. Eros is beyond the structure of narcissism, not its equivalent.

I've been asked many times by students and psychoanalysts why Lacan insists on the question of lack and absence, as opposed to say the good breast or the ego. Desire, for Lacan, cannot be separated from lack. The image of the potter with the hole around which he fashions his object is one crucial example. There are many ways I hope to show you the virtues of taking psychoanalysis from this angle of a centralized emptiness. In particular, how it aims to cut through the traps of narcissism, wed to a formalism that is closer to the structure and logic of the unconscious as Freud theorized it in his *metapsychology*.

Many strains of psychoanalytic thought positively render the relationship between our clinical work and the question of mastery—what Freud refers to as *Bemachtigungstrieb* or the drive for mastery. It is not so uncomplicated. Substituting mastery for genuine questions of epistemology is a substitution that I think is fundamentally detrimental to the psychoanalytic project. The question of what can be known and how it can be know was raised by Freud the minute he highlighted this idea of the unconscious and unconscious desire. Epistemological questions are foundational to the clinical act; mastery is something else.

If the unconscious is not an object of mastery, then knowledge of it would have to be something different from this. How can we maintain a theory of mastery over that which resists mastery? What does it mean to delink these categories? It was Lacan's effort to rewrite or theorize the link once again between desire and knowledge, notably though his concept of the transference as one toward a *subject supposed to know*—a fantasy of mastery that is irrevocably tied to the sexual. This work turns around the importance of this question about knowledge and the problems of authority and authorship that, from my point of view, wrestle with the most crucial concepts necessary for psychoanalysis. We must find a way beyond the fantasy of knowledge as mastery.

One might say that any subversion of narcissism, the move from preoedipal, through Oedipal, to so-called "genital" sexuality, or, perhaps even more simply the possibility of sublimation as Lacan (1986/1992) defined it in the *Ethics* seminar, requires a change in the subject with respect to his relationship to knowledge. One could rightly take this to mean that there is an inherent relationship between narcissism and knowledge taken as a form of mastery. I don't think I'm the first to suggest such a thing. One might remember that Socrates himself professed to know nothing as an attempt to get around this dilemma, including in *The Symposium* the problem of the transferential love of his disciples.

It is a subject's relation to unconscious desire in the work of psychoanalysis that is able to offer the possibility of a new subjective position with respect to a knowledge he or she *does not know, cannot master*. Narcissism is certainly about ways of shoring up one's sense of self.

More important than its quality as illusory is its strategy: it is always an act of closure with respect to desire. Desire and narcissism, life and death, are the mutually opposed contenders. It is desire, buried in this way, that is the decentered center of analysis—an act that Lacan names, in particular, the analysis of hysteria.

In an intimate encounter with hysteria the knowledge of psychoanalysis is pushed. Lacan reenlarges this category back toward its critical place at the foundation of Freud's discoveries. Hysteria was *the* challenge to psychiatric medical knowledge based on an ideal of conscious mastery. Dora's final dream is close to the truth of Freud's project: in the place where she expects to find her father instead finds that he has died and settles down to read her big book on sexuality (Freud, 1905b). In the hysteric's relation to father figures she shows you the place of the abyss, the place where all conscious knowledge fails.

This failure, rather than being a limitation, becomes a new site of possibility. Certainly it was the original site of possibility for Freud's work. On the part of the analyst what is required is to understand how interpretation has effects that only border on knowledge, authority, and meaning. Doing so means to meet face to face with the hysterical demand. Notoriously difficult, a hysteric forces the position of the analyst into the narrow straights between knowledge as mastery and knowledge as truth, prompting the ethical considerations of the analytic position. We must refuse to let this question of her desire close.

The rigor of listening and the tactful handling of the transference, Lacan believed, will lead one to the right kind of failure in knowledge, meaning some truth would bring itself to bear in the analytic situation. The idea that truth comes of its own accord cannot be stressed enough. It will only come if it is not known in advance. One is literally delivered there by chance. Thus the failure to do what one intends is so important for Lacan as conscious intention invites refusal among the most hysterical—and rightfully so.

In Lacan's seminar, *Les Non-Dupes Errent*, he divides the set in half. There is being a master and there is being a dupe (Lacan, 1973). Perhaps analysts, like the Jack of all trades, learn the art of mastering nothing, always following blindly this trail of desire. "You'll be fine," Lacan reassures, or, at the very least better off than being the nondupe who always makes a mistake. Failure is never failure pure and simple in psychoanalysis. The unconscious is what arrives when intentions fail, it is what passes us by, what we stumble and limp after. The analyst, he says, is a glorious fool. Nothing is stupider than inhibition for Lacan except perhaps the psychoanalyst! I find these words a strange comfort.

To return to the question of weariness, a fatigue no doubt coming from the expectation of mastery, it is through Lacan that I find a way to slow down. This is an important moment. One *must* be fatigued. It is a necessary first step. It is a weariness that takes into consideration how radically threatened we are as a community. It is one that acknowledges the thrilling groundlessness of our work. Doing so, it forms itself around a question, not an answer. Mastery is thereby undercut (or so I hope) as the means of the social bond between psychoanalysts. Our own origin—as a question about desire, not mastery—can become the point of orientation. We are the forever strange discipline that maintains its tie to its parent Freud in a question about desire that is filtered through his own. We must, perhaps wearily, pass through Freud.

Over one hundred years later it is undeniable that psychoanalysis is facing a crisis of legitimacy that extends to the very foundations of the ethical responsibility of its work. To ask questions about the foundations of our work seems to threaten what is already under threat externally. It does so with a strategy that takes this threat and puts it on the affirmatively precarious ground of its own unstable origins. The threat, it seems to me, can only be taken further—the answer we give to most patients who seek our help. There is no other means of escaping the hypocrisy of a premature answer.

I will try to situate the question of psychoanalysis as best that I can around this act of questioning—what does it mean to desire psychoanalysis? Counter to the letter in my dream of the vase, a letter addressed to no one, in the end uncirculated and unopened, I will try and open the question of psychoanalysis outward. I will take my lesson from Freud. He did not fulfill his phantasm to be the first and final transgressor, master of the unconscious, but rather moved through this into his passion for discovery, courage against authority, and fidelity to truth. Passion, courage, and fidelity are different kinds of virtue than the ones that rest on any imagined solid ground.

That all this is bound up with the idea that we must traverse the transference is certainly a major force within this work. Even further, there is in psychoanalysis a fragile moment of submission, a giving in to fatigue, to the threat, to a dream—touching impossibility. As Freud

declared to Fliess during a critical moment in his self-analysis, *I now feel
a void*. In the face of this abyss he discovered a certain kind of courage.
That we must find the same courage is the impossibility on which this
work rests. So when I asked before in the preface of this work, "do I
fail?", the answer is, of course I do, with pleasure. May this pleasure be
directed against the conceit of my wishful dream.

If psychoanalysis is on the verge of death, it will be from having
lost its passion, its Eros that was always both its origin and its aim.
Knowledge is drained of Eros in order to pledge a future that belongs
to no-one. Psychoanalysis was always a hollowed out promise, mere
words, which cannot sustain themselves without submitting to this
passion for being, passion always being something precarious. Herein
resides the space of my invitation.

This invitation carries with it the possibility of its demise, its double. If the vase was this invitation, it brought with it the letter and the
commandment. The letter mirrored this promise but one whose pledge
brought certainty and closure. Certainty can come in the form of objec-
tified knowledge. My Grandmother's commandment is fulfilled in its
inverted form—not master of none, one master, one memory. There is
nothing but the desire for psychoanalysis to continue.

ADORNO

Disenchantment and love

After all of this talk about psychoanalysis it seems strange to turn to someone so distant from its practice as the philosopher Theodor Adorno. He is, to my mind, the great synthesizer of Marx, Freud, and Nietzsche, marking the juncture between Freud's time and ours. He takes Freud and translates his work into a critical theory that lives up to its name. Adorno is not only critical in the dynamic sense, he is so by nature—cranky, authoritarian, and discontent. Perhaps he lives out a discontent, a malaise stemming from civilization, that Freud only begins to point to.

Adorno's thought exists on a terrain such that he always knows what is good, bad, tasteful, degraded, the right questions to ask, the ways of rigor, what is necessary, what is impossible, and never, ever, for a moment positing what is. The possible is an offense after the events of World War II. He is one of those philosophers who pointedly absorbed the trauma of the two world wars, wars that were also of major consequences for the birth of the psychoanalytic institution. We must put into perspective a modernity that Adorno sees as culminating in the events of the holocaust.

14

To my mind, Adorno is an important figure to wrestle with. He pushes the consequences of what he calls the fundamental disenchantment of the world that reaches its peak in the 20th century—a disenchantment that is not so distant from what Freud calls neurosis or modern nervous illness. For Adorno, the history of mankind is the history of the withdrawal of truth, authentic experience, and ethical life, and Adorno proffers to his readers the intricacy of their entanglement in this barbarism: we sanction the withdrawal. Our existence is coextensive with a fundamentally uncharitable existence. Our sentiment is always already false sentiment.

In this extreme disenchantment, of necessity pointing to the very problematic disenchantment of the world, I see in Adorno a driving hope and an unrelenting love. Adorno writes about what he loves in absolute *negation*. What does it mean to hold on to love through negativity? Does it not mirror the very act of disenchantment as the most powerful enchantment? As Cavell said (1979), romantics dream revolution and break their hearts. Reading Adorno is like reading the work of the heart-broken and betrayed.

I loved Adorno more than any other thinker, even Lacan. This love affair lasted almost a decade. I am not sure I can love a thinker in the same way anymore—with such slavish devotion—and I am not sure I even know why that has come to pass or whether I should be grateful for that passing. Nevertheless I know it has occurred and I fault my analysis of almost exact duration. Something in analysis changed my relation not only to Adorno, but also what I look for in relation to knowledge; what I hear in the written voice of an author. While this is certainly a chapter on the question of Adorno, it is perhaps above all a chapter on how my relation to Adorno changed during this period of time, situating the difference between his work and the question of psychoanalysis.

Adorno makes an irresistible promise to his readers one that I had for a time taken in. In his last lecture from *The Problems of Moral Philosophy* given in 1963, he states:

> On the question of whether moral philosophy is possible today, the only thing I would be able to say is that essentially it would consist in the attempt to make conscious the critique of moral philosophy .... More than this, I believe, cannot in all decency be promised. Above all, no one can promise that the reflections that

> can be entertained in the realm of moral philosophy can be used
> to establish a canonical plan for the good life *because* life itself is
> so deformed and distorted that no one is able to live the good life
> in it or to fulfill his destiny as a human being (Adorno, 1996/2000,
> p. 167).

Adorno's position is an unremitting consciousness of impotence. Reflectivity can lead to no prescription for action or redemption. Belief is always already denial. The circle is closed. I think one can love Adorno for so thoroughly closing it in the way that he does throughout his work, from one end of it to the other.

Exile is always a virtue. Hope must be shrouded in this act of errant desperation. This is the way to be nonviolent. Adorno's philosophy as a philosophy of disenchantment is wed to the stated impossibility of transformative action or revelation. One buries the object of hope in order to bring about a fuller awareness of the world in all its contradictions. Idealism bad, materialism good, I was taught.

Psychoanalysis takes this impossibility differently. While Adorno's philosophy positions the object as having vanished, nonexistent, and asks that one not force this object to exist (that would be to do violence to that which has already been subjugated), for psychoanalysis, this protection doesn't necessarily reckon with the object as lost. Or, to put it another way, the object as lost is not only a source of damage. The lost object in psychoanalysis, in fact, must *be* irrevocably lost. Its loss is the condition of subjectivity, desire, and speech.

Adorno's nonexistent object, while reckoning with its absence, is nonetheless given greater and greater imaginary materiality and consistency. The object becomes something nearly impossible to lose, and instead, it is posited as something to cling to. In Adorno's *because,* in the quote from *The Problems of Moral Philosophy,* he establishes the why of its impossibility—Why? Because. *No one can.* There is a force of certainty that holds onto this object in a negation that ultimately negates its own quality of loss. It is the double negation of a kind of hopeless romanticism.

Why does Adorno assume here that he knows with so much certainty when he allows almost nothing the same claim? This certainty fulfills the promise of impotence. It is true that reflection cannot be used to establish a canonical plan. It is as well true that life is deformed. But the causal link is *not* certain, its ubiquity even less so. And who, in any case, asked for this canonical plan?

Even if instrumental reason, along with a burgeoning relativism that opposes that reason, grow absolute, Adorno's certainty about absolutism is itself absolute. I think it is for this that I loved him without question. He promised nothing and yet in a very subtle way, I think you can see that he promises almost everything. Is this not what every hysteric loves? The object proffered to her at a distance? The distance as what purifies her demand?

What Adorno does not have is always a lament. Despair, melancholia, damage, give the lie and function as orienting signs. Adorno's incredible gift is to think thought in contradiction, aporia, and failure, without a doubt the result of going to the heart of what he calls the damaged life. No one escapes failure, and yet, he likewise makes constant demands that one, at some point, be able to, negating the significance of this recognition. Failure is always external and too real. The memory of injury is the best of all possible objects for Adorno.

I cannot but see this as running counter to the basic affirmation of the universality of failure in Freud—an intimate ethic that I see underlying his body of work. It was through the *abnormal*, the aberrations, that Freud defined the space of the normal. The unconscious is our great equalizer. I think, and I hope I will show, that this is why the object is not lamented in its nonexistence but celebrated in its absence or loss. Making failure universal does not sanction violence; it is an attempt to counter it. That we may finally be able to rest on this point of emptiness is the perhaps indecent promise of the psychoanalyst.

Adorno is never master of this none, but master of one—one life, one object, one faith, one failure. Good that he's got it under his control. Terrible that this was exactly what he wanted to avoid. When I think of this "more" of his—"more than this, I believe, cannot in all decency be promised"—it is hard for me to imagine what this more could possibly be. What more *he* imagined here and backed away from.

This is nowhere clearer than in *Minima Moralia (1951/1974)*. Flashes of possibility are constantly torn asunder. Not by inevitability, but by Adorno himself. Any imagined possibility was too much for Adorno. He preferred to keep his desire mired to impossibility—a fantasy of fulfillment that is always deferred. "No poetry after Auschwitz," as his famous declaration goes.

Adorno never really maintained a faith in language, in the possibility of speech, perhaps just silent resistance, isolated reflexivity, at best conscious nonparticipation. In the end, I think his only consolation was music where he cordoned off his hope and his Eros. Compartmentalization leads down the path of an impossible and impossibly virulent arrogance, born from the most desperate hope, out of an entirely sanctioned pain. This is Freud's failed neurotic rebellion. I always forgave Adorno his essay on jazz when I would never forgive others for so much less.

For the love of Hegel

Love has a certain power for Lacan as the transformative lever of the transference. Through the transference, work on what tends toward violence, repetition, narcissism, and the instrumentality of the pleasure principle, is given momentum. How? Only through an act of careful listening. It is for this reason that I find Adorno (1963/1993) at his best in a strange essay of his, *Skoteinos, or How to Read Hegel*. His love for Hegel manifests itself in his pure desire to have you listen to his words—huge quotations without explanation. They go on for pages.

If one has read Adorno, it is uncanny to encounter these endless citations and his almost spoken words to his reader: "read, it's good, I promise, keep reading, it'll be worth it, wait, be patient." Adorno's wish is for Hegel to appear in the very formation of his sentences and the march of his thought, something more than just failure and bad equivocation as marked by Hegel's critics. Hegel, he will say, lets go of something, akin to systematization, but Adorno is trying to understand how it is also something more than just that. Furthermore, he is beginning to ask what this has to do with language and with writing.

Adorno becomes interested in the "suspended quality associated with Hegel's philosophy" (Adorno, 1963/1993, p. 91) what is at stake in Hegel's writing and its unfolding dialectic. This is also, of course, the moment before Hegel lapses into his greatest falsity according to Adorno: when the *Phenomenology* concludes on the perverse note of absolute knowledge. But here, through Hegel's words, one is asked to make allowances. Every sentence is unsuitable to its aim. Exceeds it in fact. To allow for this excess is to read with a generosity of spirit.

Adorno is patient with Hegel. There is work to be done! There is an intention of the whole, but it is not this whole but the work done in that direction which makes up the moments of understanding. He displaces the final aim as, perhaps, a necessary fantasy. In this kind of work, the whole, this end, can become an untruth that does not thereby render the work false. If anything, it gives it its truth all the more:

> Hegel makes himself inaccessible to anyone who is not familiar with his overall intention .... At every point one must bear in mind, however provisionally, what Hegel is after; one must illuminate him from behind, so to speak .... But if one stakes everything on this one can falsify him again. One then easily creates what has thus far been injurious to interpretation, namely, an empty consciousness of the system that is incompatible with the fact that the system is not intended to form an abstract higher-order concept with regard to its moment but rather to achieve its truth only in and through the concrete moments" (Adorno, 1963/1993, p. 92).

To illuminate from behind is to play without injuring the possibility for interpretation, without the stakes becoming too high, too concrete, too essential, nor, too abstract, too empty, or too distant. This play with a demand that forces one to go to work in tension with false intentions is the play of reading Hegel.

He picks up a dual demand—"to float along, to let himself be borne by the current and not to force the momentary to linger," as well as, to "develop an intellectual slow-motion procedure, to slow down the tempo at the cloudy places in such a way that they do not evaporate and their motion can be seen" (Adorno, 1963/1993, p. 123). The reading, just as the content read, is split into extremes: slow/fast, concrete/abstract. Balancing these extremes is part of the work in an encounter with another's work.

Adorno contrasts this kind of reading with one that he calls *fetishistic*. The fetishistic demand is a demand that the work one is delivered be complete. This is always a kind of false consciousness. It leaves out the necessity of time articulated in the distinction between what is familiar and what is not yet familiar, what already exists and what is new—a temporal organizing in a dialectic of *retroactive force* and *retrogressive consciousness*. This is to listen with a *speculative ear*. In wanting to keep things freed from time's articulation, the speculative ear runs deaf.

The work must be bound by the play of the language one hears, not the imperative of knowledge or the claim that one wants to make on another's final or initial intent. There is a rhythm of opening and closing. He will say that Hegel's ideal is *nonargumentative thought*, a philosophy "of identity stretched to the breaking point" where relaxation must be retained (Adorno, 1963/1993, p. 141). In reading Hegel nonargumentatively, flashes of illumination will appear that cannot be extinguished. It's a wonderful moment in Adorno whereby a moment has the possibility of redemption.

Adorno seems to stumble upon Hegel's language, developing a theory of expression before he will write his final, posthumously published work, *Aesthetic Theory (1969/1997)*. This reading of Hegel will form part of the basis of his argument on the play of forces at work in the art object. For Adorno we must try to give voice to the inexpressible—situating it as the evanescent itself, the object driven away by the violence of thought and the instrumental tension of reason.

One realizes the fragility of sensuous life. Both intellectual abstraction and brute materiality refuse this fragility, no less sensuality. The object as one that is lost resists expression. This resistance doesn't have to be merely a source of nostalgia. It can also be a way of locating a possible place for contact with whatever sensuality is left to us, even if that is only the expression of the pain experienced at these very limits. This possibility is a very different one from the Adorno of the impossibility of moral philosophy or the good life.

But a question remains for me. How can Adorno understand the necessity to put aside demands upon language for clarity, identity stretched to the breaking point, when he will then condescend to a belief that there can be, at some point, some correspondence with actuality? Adorno will always grow argumentative. Adorno's most stringent disciples are ruthlessly argumentative, critical, and knowing.

These moments his aesthetics theorize are eclipsed by this knowing edge. The evanescent is fundamentally contradicted. Adorno will say with consternation that Hegel, in the end, destroys his own work. He makes do with declarations: "theses that say that something is so when the work has not yet been done" (Adorno, 1963/1993, p. 94). Like father, like son, Jack of all trades, master of none.

Hegel, Adorno says, does not allow something into his own language. He sides too much with objectivity: "what gives it that air [of sovereignty] is the preponderance of quasi-oral delivery over the written text. Vagueness, something that cannot be eliminated in dialectic, becomes a defect in Hegel because he did not include an antidote to it in his language" (Adorno, 1963/1993, p. 100). He looms too large in his own text. Is it not the same with Adorno? Adorno who—while creating the paratactic antidote, his particular writing style—dictates to his wife his work, *Aesthetic Theory*, during the last years of his life back in Germany?

Such a strange scene: this philosopher and his stenographer wife. The book is almost unreadable. Adorno's labor would also come to overshadow his work too much, bringing this movement he so carefully details to a halt. In a moment of great irony Adorno writes, "the art of reading [Hegel] should take note of where something new begins, some content, and where a machine that was not intended to be a machine is simply running and ought not to keep doing so" (Adorno, 1963/1993, p. 95).

I will read to see where the machine that never should have been a machine is simply running and ought not to keep doing so, loving him as much as he continued to love Hegel, beyond false intent, for whatever he can bring of the new. It is a love that tries to stay the slide onto the side of repetition, desperate to slow down the movement to the moment between beats—near silence and with pause. Adorno's time will soon come. From one side, I cannot slow it down enough. From yet another, it is also true that I could not have precipitated the crossing fast enough.

When I read Adorno, I see that he wanted to stay in this before, this silence, because he knew it would lapse. Adorno ends this essay saying that Hegel's work "says, with pathos, nonidentity .... The dialectic could be consistent only in sacrificing consistency by following its own logic to the end. These, and nothing less, are the stakes in understanding Hegel" (Adorno, 1963/1993, p. 148). It is the term sacrifice that fascinates me.

Adorno declares that Hegel is inconsistent in his attempt to achieve a consistency without true sacrifice. What is *true* sacrifice? Adorno lays emphasis less on the nature of this sacrifice than on the situation as one of mere *pathos*. He doesn't seem able to draw out his own conclusion. What we know about this sacrifice is that it concerns a sacrifice of one's own consistency or desire for integrity. Drawing out one's logic to its very end involves a significant risk and wager. "A subject's nonidentity without sacrifice would be utopian" (Adorno, 1966/1973, p. 281).

Desire, as Lacan understood it, is a movement that works in and through risk and failure. Desire bears an intrinsic relation with loss, with the delicate history of one's most intimate and frightening wishes.

It is this movement of desire that the neurotic cannot bear. Paralysis, dissatisfaction, complaint, feels more secure than this work with desire. Underneath this inhibition, as with Freud, lies a greediness that knows no obstacles.

While I read this essay of Adorno's, I hear in him as he reads Hegel the movement of analysis as I have come to understand it through Lacan. Adorno, with Hegel, out of love for Hegel, allowed himself momentarily to be a dupe. When he lapses from this position as *dupe*, I hear the dangers of analysis taken too far—interpretation as a knowing argument. While Adorno ends in a place that I have come to criticize, he nevertheless embodies in this essay the patience necessary in any reading and any listening taken on without any certainty.

I hear his demand. What he wants must *be* so in reality. His knowledge increases in proportion with this growing demand. Likewise I refuse this demand (how can I but not). While there may not be an immediate return or a future guarantee there is a promise that can be made to continue to listen. This is a promise that refuses knowledge, refuses to declare either the demand or the world on which it is turned unfit, and thereby to listen to what is beyond it.

The object will not be relegated to an elsewhere or given status in the beyond—it will be nowhere in as much as one comes to know that this object is the obstacle not the solution. It is for this reason that the analyst, for Lacan, must fall. You need the analyst to know that you do not need them any longer—you have to risk desiring them to find out that to have them is to lose them. I had to assume that Adorno knew without question in order to find my position as a subject who is allowed knowledge in her own right. I needed Adorno in order to say to you now that I do not need him any longer. Perhaps if there is anything we know it is that this is both the risk of love and the bearing-out of disenchantment.

So it stands that where I failed for all these years with Adorno was to refuse to know where Adorno disappointed me. I think I can say to you that I erred in faith not bad conscience. The place of knowledge was left open just enough—hysterical ignorance out of hysterical reverence. I never got as far as my own certainty, just an identification with his. So one has to wait, hope, for a passing, for the fall. The letter was but a dream and a wish that can be brought under question.

Adorno is the supposed subject of knowledge situated in the place of the analyst in the transference. He couldn't resist taking up this position. For a time, face to face with his silence, his impossible desire, his certainty—I would remain utterly ignorant. So I had to find a way to read him as he read Hegel, looking for what is new out of what is old and should not continue running. It was through Lacan that I found the means of doing so.

Now there are two. I am better off with both of them, reverence split between Adorno and Lacan. Adorno who I loved without question, and the form it takes now, after Lacan. Being overpowered by Adorno's system may be as much from my own phantasy as that which dictated his path. Don't we always locate these points of correspondence in those we read so intimately? Be patient with me. Wait before you throw your hands up in the face of what seems like the inevitable distortions of love. We might arrive somewhere quite unexpected.

Sentimentality, semblance, sublimation

Adorno states in *Minima Moralia*, "if today the subject is vanishing, aphorisms take upon themselves the duty to consider the evanescent itself as essential" (Adorno, 1951/1974, p. 16). Where Adorno leaves off in raising to its apogee this question of the revolutionary character of the evanescent moment one can find Lacan in the running. The evanescent *is* desire. And it is always this that the hysteric chases as a question about her own being. What woman is and what does woman want collapse around this point of desire that is more her than she knows. It was Lacan's genius to describe the evanescent in a curious equivalence between the unconscious as nonidentity, and woman as Other. This is, of course, a rather strange equivalence, but perhaps with Adorno we should admit that "in psychoanalysis, nothing is true except the exaggerations" (Adorno, 1951/1974, p. 49).

Adorno never really had faith in the practice, no less the institution, of psychoanalysis. His criticisms are well founded. "Psychoanalysis itself," he says, "is castrated by its conventionalization: sexual motives, partly disavowed and partly approved are made totally insignificant .... The last grandly conceived theorem of bourgeois self-criticism has become a means of making bourgeois self-alienation, in its final phase, absolute, and of rendering ineffectual the lingering awareness of the ancient wound in which lies hope of a better future" (Adorno, 1951/1974, p. 66). Psychoanalysis as a theory or practice is no longer critical of alienation but emblematic of it—a therapeutic celebration of reflexive individuality. The only hope is the wound itself, our last site of contact with the sensuous life of desire in its damaged form. Psychoanalysis, far from addressing this, glosses it in its utter conventionality.

Beyond what he specifically says about psychoanalysis it is more the question of this wound, for Lacan always feminine, that I find the greatest correspondence between Adorno's thought and psychoanalysis. If Adorno is right that the authority of the analyst should return to the authority of this ancient wound, it is not however purely because of its veracity. For Lacan, the question of the wound is something like a first step—a kind of hystericization of discourse that splits it right down the middle like a massive gash. Words are given life by virtue of being able to sustain this tension. The wound is only a way station to desire.

Lacan, taking off from Hegel, points out that the hysteric cannot exit from her system of accusation, centered on this wound. The beautiful soul is she who fails to recognize the disorder in herself that she bemoans. Work with her is work with bringing her closer to this truth— one might say the truth of her split-wounded subjectivity. The hope is a hope that what may come of this contact with the wound would be a rekindling of Eros.

I was surprised to find that what Adorno says about love is not so indistinguishable from Lacan; that around this question of the wounds of love and the love of wounds, they seem to meet in fascinating ways. Lacan famously said that *to love is to give what one does not have*, using love as a psychoanalyst should, contextualized by loss. And the soul, Adorno says, dawns on love only in its absence. "Soul itself is the longing of the soulless for redemption" (Adorno, 1951/1974, p. 170). Love is there "only where you may show yourself weak without provoking strength" (Adorno, 1951/1974, p. 192). They both play so beautifully with the loss and longing, pain and nostalgia, that is inseparable from loving.

The timbre of these reflections center on the negative sensuousness of love—its impossible yearning for what has already been bartered away or lost. What is gained is always gained too late or where it no longer counts in the way one wants. Love is the gift of this weakness. While love in Lacan forms the very center and crux of his thought, in Adorno it is only one among many passing reflections, not entirely without bearing, but quickly overridden.

Love, which takes on so many guises in psychoanalytic work, is for Lacan that which points in the direction of a potential sacrifice, the sacrifice of what he calls *jouissance*, or, the insular enjoyment of our symptoms. The patient transfers onto the analyst all the vicissitudes of a repeatable fantasy that sustains their *jouissance* and blocks access to desire. Only then can the historical truth of the analysand, embedded in their symptom, perhaps be unraveled. Through analytic work—the staging of the fantasy—*jouissance* potentially gives way to the unique and singular desire that sustains a patient's relation to the world. We saw this in miniature in Leclaire's analysis of Freud.

This relay between desire and *jouissance* is also the task Adorno leaves to love in *Minima Moralia*:

> If people were no longer possessions they could no longer be exchanged. True affection would be one that speaks specifically to the other, and becomes attached to a beloved feature and not to the idol of personality, the reflected image of possession. The specific is not exclusive: it lacks the aspiration towards totality. But, in another sense it is exclusive, nevertheless; the experience indissolubly bound up with it does not indeed forbid replacement, but by its very essence precludes it. The protection of anything quite definite is that it cannot be repeated which is just why it tolerates what is different (Adorno, 1951/1974, p. 79).

I find this passage remarkable. Adorno knew his Freud well and seems to follow his thoughts in *On Narcissism (1914)* where he discerns the libidinal difference between the act of loving and the act of being loved. The more narcissistic the love the more the object exists solely as a prop for the self, a support for a fantasy. The specificity of desire, of what one loves in a beloved, is the only antidote to this utilitarian relationship to the other.

Love, for Adorno, potentially moves beyond the aspiration to totality or total possession. Love is attached to the other in their radical difference from oneself. True love, like true sacrifice in Adorno's reading of Hegel, holds to a relationship that abandons the need for self-consistency. The fetishistic demand is overturned. These reflections on love in Adorno are not, however, a theoretical work on the question of desire, no less an insistence on what it promises. They are only a way station for his reflections on the realm of the aesthetic. This is particularly true in his late work.

Nonetheless, this movement he delineates from sentimentality, to love, to the realm of the aesthetic, seems to me close to the very path of sublimation itself. What Freud always indicated by *love and work* were those areas of life, at a remove from the constraints of self-preservation, that require something of a transformation of desire. *Jouissance* tends to treat the object as one closer to an object of need without any inherent particularity to that object beyond its quality as sating. Sublimation requires a sacrifice of *jouissance,* or, as Lacan put it, a renunciation of *jouissance* so that it can condescend to the inverted ladder of desire.

The difference between a theory of desire and an aesthetic theory is perhaps minimal. Or, to render the question more positively, what they share is important, hinging on a question of representation in relation to desire. Art for Adorno is a realm in which truth might appear precisely because it is has no real substantial value. It can engage us at our boundary points, the limit between inside and outside, the visible and invisible, individual and broader culture. Life, dragged down to the level of brute need makes the realm of aesthetic truth a necessity in its very superfluity. Aesthetics is a reawakening of truth in an act that runs counter to this thread of bare isolated and anesthetic life, providing, for Adorno, the missing cross roads.

Lacan as well, when he tries to imagine the possibility of what psychoanalysis preserves, gives an answer that I think is close to Adorno's elevation of the realm of aesthetics in this regard. If there is no good life in the false one, psychoanalysis offers the possibility of a private life—a curious term indeed—where Lacan locates the greatest potential for creation. Private life is the place of private fictions. Not only can one see the effect they hold over us, we might, for once, not delude ourselves about the fictive, created, perhaps aesthetic, nature of our lives. We might then find some room for play and invention.

So there is something about this private sphere where private sexuality and cultural necessity irrevocably cross. Lacan says:

> Private means everything that preserves on this delicate point of
> what is involved in the sexual act and of everything that flows from
> it, in the pairing of individuals, in the "you are my wife, I am your

husband" and other essential devices on another register that we know well, namely that of fiction. This is what allows there to hold up in a field in which we analysts introduce an order of relativity which, as you see, is not at all easy to master; and which can be mastered on a single condition, If we are able to recognize the place we hold in it, we, as analysts, not as analysts who are a subject of knowledge but as analysts who are instruments of revelation (Lacan, 1967, Lecture XV, p. 18).

Like Freud's act of loosening the bond between drive and object in the *Three Essays on the Theory of Sexuality (1905a)*, it gives new meaning to the idea of creation—the constructed nature of the object of desire. We must recognize the place we hold in it, and only then, the further possibilities we can make of it.

Semblance, fiction, can have just as much bearing as the long sought after thing-in-itself. This is perhaps one truth that Lacan and Adorno incontestably share. This is the precarious advantage afforded the analyst who doesn't need to play a game of knowledge or determine the reality of a given situation. The analyst plays a game of revelation— this delicate point where all that flows from the sexual defines the place of possibility. It is, to my mind, a powerful redefinition of sublimation. It is also the revolutionary potential that Adorno sees in great works of art.

Adorno's claim then is that semblance disenchants the disenchanted world. It is not so far from Lacan for whom semblance restores the possibility of a private life, particularly through the reenchanting power of language, restoring to words their magic which has been diluted by daily life. If nonidentity is the vain pursuit of the artwork and the vain pursuit of psychoanalysis, in vain they must manage. Both are removed from the constraints of self-preservation, making room for some new possibility within the impossibility of a form of work that has no supposed value in the world of things—a work of art in a utilitarian world, a patient taking time to speak to another in an uneconomical way.

It is precisely for this reason that Lacan says the analyst has no private life with respect to his analysands—this enabling their own. This "inhumanity" of the analyst allows another face of the human to appear. In fact, against the desperate human link in the dream of *the letter and the vase*, Laplanche makes a similar claims in *Life and Death in Psychoanalysis*, among other works. For Laplanche, only with the analyst in the place of the most extreme Otherness, as a *provocateur*, can psycho-analysis transform the economics of the drive. The drive for Laplanche is propped up on and yet incommensurate with the language of need or self-preservation—what he calls the more human side. The drive, maintaining this liminal space, produces a place of possible refuge for the subject in something entirely anonymous, something entirely Other (Laplanche, 1999).

Likewise, Rieff (1959) will call Freud's concept of the drive dynamic and critical; and for this, he calls Freud the most populous, moral, and intimate of the modern thinkers. In the Freudian system the drive takes what is biological and inserts it into the sphere of subjectivity. It is only in this narrow and narrowly defined realm that one can find a defense against repressive culture. What is most extimate—biology—is shown as wholly intimate to subjectivity. Thus sexuality is not only a problem, indeed it is, but it contains the only solution to a subjectivity hemmed in on all sides.

In Laplanche's and Rieff's conceptualization, the external response to a subject can only but fail. In fact, it must fail. The object, as we said before, is lost. There is not a perfect match between this inner life of desire and the object it seeks externally. It is only through a radical conceptualization of this failure that we move away from, for Reiff, blaming society in a deluded liberal hopefulness, or maintaining a fundamentally normative, and hence moralistic, conception of a subject. Subjectivity begins with this internal failure and only within that fail-ure locates possibility—what I think both would consider sublimation. Any other conceptualization will run straight into the aporia of diluting sexuality in order to rescue either an eternal subject (Jung) or an eternal reality construed as utopia (Adler).

Sublimation requires this failure. Perhaps the link between sublima-tion and the revolutionary character of the artwork has some valid-ity after all. We escape domination through a kind of uncolonizable sexuality. It is through desire that we get as close as we can to the thing, *das Ding*, for Lacan—and we do so through semblance. We raise the object, as Lacan says, to the dignity of the thing. Nonidentity is sub-jectively held in place and given back its possibility by the Freudian drive.

For Adorno, the artwork demands nonidentity—a truth that springs from a subject—attempting to overturn the situation where the subject is the condition for the vanishing of the object. In Adorno's *Aesthetic*

Theory (1969/1997) the pursuit of nonidentity means that the artwork must go beyond itself, threatening its own internal consistency. In Lacanian terms, one risks death in the liquidation of all anchoring points that shore up the subject: "the most enduring result of Hegelian logic is that the individual is not flatly for himself. In himself, he is otherness and linked with others. What is, is more than it is. This *more* is not imposed upon it but what remains immanent to it, as that which has been pushed out of it. In that sense, the nonidentical would be the thing's own identity against its identifications" (Adorno, 1969/1997, p. 174). The power of the artwork is that it confronts us with the sublime as the realm that is always beyond our own narcissism. What is, as he says, is more than it is.

Thus aesthetic experience is the experience of letting the self, self-preservation, fall away. Although it does not completely succeed in realizing this potential, the potential is experienced. This movement, Adorno says, shatters conscious experience of the self as ultimate and absolute. The sublime experience contains both the primal feelings of powerlessness—in Kant, weakness before natural beauty—and, the demonic feelings of omnipotence. The first is given back its existence in consciousness (as natural experience), as the second is stripped of its existence as consciousness (as unnatural experience). This is for Adorno the sublime trembling between nature and freedom, determination and will. We should, I think, hear sublimation in this reevocation of the Kantian concept of the Sublime.

While the cure for sickness for Adorno was always the necessity that it grow worse, that the wounds inflicted by humanity continue to fester and torment our psyche—lest one escape into innocence—here we might see how the symptom builds up in tension in order to fall out. The symptom contains the very means of its own transformation. Lacan uses the word semblance as a synonym for the symptom—a fiction whose truth is more powerful than any supposed reality. The symptom literally causes one to shudder and tremble, like in so many hysterics.

Semblance has the power to heal the unhealable wound with the spear that inflicted it. I can't think of anything else more poignantly asked for by a hysteric. Art is the ever broken promise of happiness for Adorno, and perhaps to analyze the hysteric is to make her put to use this ever-broken promise rather than give in to "the ecstasy of sacrifice where delusion recognizes its own humiliation and becomes equal to the enormity of domination that in real life it is powerless to overcome" (Adorno, 1951/1974, p. 66). Again, semblance disenchants the disenchanted world.

Nevertheless, I would say that in the end, with Adorno, this aim is ultimately submerged under a final aim, which is always aesthetic theory itself. We must, Adorno says, transform the semblance of the work of art into thought. It is, at this point, that I can follow Adorno no longer—this need for meta-interpretation, no less the must of his must transform. The play of semblance is not discontinuous from truth or thought. This play, as in clinical work, is often enough. Ask any psychoanalyst who works with children whether a child who plays doesn't always already know the power of what he or she is in the midst of communicating. I cannot abide by this separation between thought and action.

Adorno's *Aesthetic Theory* was left unfinished. In this strange work of sprawling dictation, it leaves you waiting on the precipice. Psychoanalysis, for my part, cannot culminate in an after-thought, in this act of recoil at the edge. What is most interesting about symptoms is that they contain their very own solution; their elucidation in analysis is their unraveling. One might say we stay with the *sickness growing worse*, which has resonance with Lacan's late seminar ... *Ou Pire*, ... Or Worse (1971b).

Adorno sees with his critical edge what he has no power to overcome, like patients well aware of their own patterns they hardly but fail not to repeat. It is as hard to read, as it is to hear:

> Fantasy alone, today consigned to the realm of the unconscious and proscribed from knowledge as a childish, injudicious rudiment, can establish that relation between objects which is the irrevocable source of all judgment: should fantasy be driven out, judgment too, the real act of knowledge is exorcised. But the castration of perception by a court of control that denies it any anticipatory desire, forces it thereby into a pattern of helplessly reiterating what is already known ... Once this last trace of emotion has been eradicated, nothing remains of thought but absolute tautology (Adorno, 1966/1973, p. 123).

Adorno, despite being able to articulate the necessity of fantasy, semblance, aesthetics—where we can find this last trace of emotion—will isolate himself from its power of judgment. Fantasy and desire seem too irrational in his fear of the irrational, bound by his fear of domination. Without this, everything *is* tautology.

What does Adorno want?

Sentimentality, fear, sadness, is a failure with respect to the life of desire. Like the hysterical fantasy that one can be loved without the risk of desire—the nostalgia for better days is never far off. "It becomes a matter of plucking the fixity and magnetism of the death drive out from recollection; of wresting from sadness its false morality, as Lacan calls it" (Miele, 2011). Desire holds on to more possibility. It allows for a different economy, a different mode of exchange. As Moustapha Safouan will say *In Praise of Hysteria*, the dream of a desire born of love "can only sharpen the antinomy between love and desire" (Safouan, 1980, p. 58).

The question of love and desire is a question I have been asking of Adorno from the beginning. Love in the hysteric is the "fibers of being tending toward an object" (Safouan, 1980). This object, as psychoanalysis has understood it, "brings no plentitude, no satisfaction" and love is this frustration. At its root, love "is annulment and abandonment, to say nothing of destruction by the object" (Safouan, 1980, p. 58). In *On Narcissism (1914)*, Freud states that the ego, in the act of loving, must bear a kind of depletion. This depletion is different from narcissistic love that seeks a return from the object. The latter would be closer to Lacan's definition of love, and the former, desire. Freud goes on to wonder if this depletion, this cost, in loving is at the root of the structure of sublimation.

This cost, dare I say sacrifice, is one that the hysteric cannot often endure. It is here where she recoils before the act. And yet, Lacan says that the hysteric knows the value of desire over love, even if in her hysteria she aims not to know it. He says that in experience love and desire are two very different things and it is always she who tells us about this difference:

> She knows very well the value of desire, namely … desire has a relationship to being, even in it's most limited, it's most shortsighted and fetishistic, let us say the word, its most stupid form … that woman will attach the value of final proof that it is indeed to her that he addresses himself … it nevertheless remains that if a man desires another woman, and that she knows that even if what the

man loves is only her slipper, the hem of her dress, or the paint that
she puts on her face, it is here that the homage to being is produced
(Lacan, 1958, L6.3.59, pp. 402–403).

So the hysteric's love always borders on this lie, or rather, it is here
that the hysteric lies about love. Lacan, it must be said, loves the hysteric and returns psychoanalysis to her in a way no other post-Freudian
theorist has.

She teaches us, he says, about truth, that is the truth of love and
desire; the truth that truth is not the opposite of semblance but continuous with it; and the truth of the value of speech when it has bearing
on one's most intimate desires. In the hysteric's very negativity, her
woundedness, she shows us the truth of the subject. Her wounds point
to the powerful way that fictions function and fracture, delineating this
cutting edge of rhetoric as the only instrument of revelation, as Lacan
called it. Without this, we would not be able to understand the nature
of symptoms.

It was for this reason that I turned to Adorno's aesthetics for nowhere
else does he come closer to this objective power of semblance, circling
around a question of love and truth. Perhaps like a good hysteric, he
knows not what he wields. And, it is difficult to avoid falling prey to
hysterical nostalgia. The hysteric, at her worst, is always bound up with
the attempt to make love essential, for semblance to be the condition
of solid reality, even if that can be nothing more than her accusation
against it. The desire that underwrites semblance takes on the character
of a demand and stagnates there. I suppose this is the one criticism of
Adorno I hold to—a criticism of his implacable romanticism. Caught in
the traps of his own game, he laments the impossible.

In a moment of striking irony, Adorno says, contesting the value
of poetic-theology, "if every symbol symbolizes nothing but another
symbol, another conceptuality, their core remains empty" (Adorno,
1966/1973, p. 399). This emptiness, as we know, is Lacan's fundamental
affirmation; it is his theory of sublimation. The signifier, like the vase, is
this radical emptiness as the possibility of creation. We cannot abandon
the characteristics of the signifier for the sake of something more full,
for the sake of some supposed *reality*. As with my dream, it is always a
fantasy of mastery.

Allow me a major divergence before concluding. One of the main
threads in the work of the classicist Nicole Loraux on Greek antiquity

(1995, 1985/1987, 1988/1998) is to etymologically deconstruct the words used in the epic poems and ancient tragedies to understand something about their guiding ethic. In elevating this play of the signifier, particularly as it approaches the themes of the body and passions, embedded in sexual or parental relations, she traces the structure of desire. Their desire is, against what many have claimed, not so far removed from our own nearly two and half thousand years later. We are, *contra* Adorno, just as disenchanted now as then. Or, perhaps better, it is not merely a question about enchantment then, disenchantment now. History comes to us through form, in particular the formal structures of language, as much then as now—telling us something different about this line between enchantment and disenchantment.

What Loraux demonstrates is that the imagery surrounding the feminine body provides *the* critical interpretive key when reading ancient Greek texts etymologically (much like Leclaire). What comes to the foreground with respect to desire, especially in the tragedies of Aeschylus, Sophocles, and Euripides, is a kind of circling around the feminine object. Helen, Medea, Antigone, Clytaemnestra, Cassandra, Electra, Hecuba, and so many others, are the major catalysts with which Athens must contend. Perhaps they are the most highly desired objects- these women are driven mad by life, stolen and exchanged, sacrificed, or even turned into conduits for the gods. As you can imagine, this makes them anything but unambivalent figures.

For Loarux, the law of the difference between the sexes is, as with any fundamental difference, a demand made upon thought. These after-waves of thought's encounter are read for the chains of meaning, the circulation of signifiers—similar to the way Freud conceptualizes the demand that the drive makes upon the mind for a certain amount of work. The law of difference is a frontier, difficult to maintain or transgress, and the signifiers for masculinity or femininity remain for the most part empty shifters. She tries to stay the impulse to over psychoanalyze. But this difference, in itself, is a means of reading: monuments of imagined bodies, lines of influence and distortion, the trace of enjoyment or anxiety, transitional spaces and modes of reversal. In short, a whole world of mythic arrangements and transmutations.

How else can we think about the body, she asks, as if thinking about the body immediately required us to think about something else. This is, she reminds us, the logic of metaphor. "With that," she says, "I would wager that it is in line with the Greeks that Freud starting with the idea of "the anatomical distinction between the sexes," created the theory of an "enlarged" sexuality extending into the realm of the psyche and a bisexuality that is at once generalized and basic to the human species, "so that the contexts of theoretical constructions of pure masculinity and pure femininity remain uncertain" (1995, p. 8). Since the feminine, like the unconscious, retains the mark of negation it becomes the richest of all possible discriminating factors.

The feminine body, acting like a negative gravitational center, poses the biggest threat to identity. Seeing this organization in the unfolding drama in the major works, Loraux defines a set of coordinates that construct a kind of Greek *ethos*. She notes that in tragedy men seem to die solely by the sword while women die of strangulation. Strangulation, in particular hanging, is the most loathsome of deaths for the Greeks who believed that the body must remain open. Like animal sacrifice, the good deaths are those that spill blood as a gift to the Gods. A good death comes in the form of an open wound. She says:

> Greek tradition is quick to contrast the wound that opens a man's body with the dangerous closure that in more than one way dooms the female body to strangulation. Perhaps, in fact, Greek thinking about the masculine finds it advantageous to close women's bodies all the better to open those of men …. This can probably be seen as a way of denying the "simple" evidence that women's bodies are inherently open-slit (Loraux, 1985/1987, p. 99).

Loraux concludes that the basic imagery that informs classical thought, even acts as its principle and most richly discriminating operator, concerns the feminine body—her body is essentially the one that is open, that sheds blood, that acts as a conduit between two necks, two mouths, the passage that essentially gives life. It is this slit/open body that supports Athenian male identity, *Andres*, where it is reappropriated. Harboring the feminine in the masculine ostensibly makes one all the more virile. The dream of feminine interiority becomes the outward banner of the glory of the *polis*. Feminine pain is transformed into the epic property of the *wounded* warrior hero. The politics of the city of Athens is defined by the military ideal of *anēr* or the glory of man in his warrior virility (Loraux, 1981/2006). Identity establishes itself with the simultaneous appropriation and negation of the feminine.

Even further, Plato, the most magnanimous culprit, banishes drama and poetry from the city as a disturbing illusion in Book X of *The Republic*—there shall be no more mimesis. It is an act of exile that Loraux cannot decouple from the important tie she establishes between tragedy and the feminine. Reflection, thought, or *logos*, is defined antithetically to the dangerous (feminine) passions. Woman, she says, is entombed in philosophy as its empty center. Woman is exiled in the name of a supposedly degendered universe that is always already masculine.

It is important to understand that Loraux does not see this as a feminist reading. She does not intend this as a polemical device in the service of anything like the equality between the sexes or a wistful return to the matriarchal. Rather, strict adherence to the law of the absolute difference between the sexes, perhaps as a placeholder for a difficult concept of difference in general, only points in the direction of a potential truth. Like trying to think about the body or sex, equality, truth, and justice must remain opaque. They are not objects of knowledge. But in rendering these objects opaque one can find one's bearings. Any *a priori* definition will preclude the capacity to continue reading.

It is this act of continuing, like an ethos of the open body, that Loraux foregrounds. Male dreams of interiority, pregnancy fantasies from Zeus onward, or the radical displacement of the feminine by *logos*, forms the nexus from which we read this feminine operator. *Anēr* is not only what defines the *polis*, but becomes the sole possibility for recognition as one of its citizens. *Anēr* is the equivalent of Athenian and the very principle of identity. In particular, it is a military identity whose glory will overthrow even death. Here, nonidentity finds once again its alliance with woman, the slave, desire, the body, and the unconscious, and nothing seems more dangerous to the unity of this *polis*.

While Adorno bemoans the violence done to all that stands outside of identity, with Loraux we locate a possibility of affirmation in reading from this empty core, even if that means only being able to read and unread a text. Like Penelope in *The Odyssey*, knowing the virtues of mobility, her desire is bound by an ethic of openness. Creation *ex nihilo*. She will weave and unweaves as she chooses. When the time comes, she will recognize her love. To the others, they die by their own sword.

CHAPTER TWO

Angels of disenchantment

I have only had three dreams which center around an object that comes under the scrutiny of my dreaming self. These objects are rare in the case of dreams and almost immediately forced me into the sudden paradox of not knowing if what I was seeing was found or created. The quality of the object as object evoked the fine line implicit in the distinction. Certainly Winnicott's (1971) transitional object is at play, an iteration of Freud's lost object refound.

Lacan will say that what designates what is most me in myself is this interior emptiness and one doesn't know if it belongs to oneself or to nobody. What is most me in myself is always something both overwhelmingly public and utterly private, problematizing the simple opposition between inside and outside. Lacan (1986/1992) creates the neologism, extimité, combining exterior and intimacy. Depth is continuous with surface, and as Freud (1919b) shows, what is most strange, uncanny (*unheimlich*), is what is revealed to be closest to home (*heim*). Adorno, I imagine, would be happy with this. Here it seems, even if only for a second, that we can overcome the division of labor. As I said, I am grateful for these dreams.

I return now to the dream that took place many years before the dream of *the vase and the letter*. This dream belongs to Adorno. That I didn't know that this dream belonged to him means that it only makes sense now, after the fact. "The landscape is barren," I used to say to my analyst. "Who said?" he would ask. "Adorno," I would answer with pride. "He has the full purchase on your reality?" he would retort. "Yes." And I would grin. This dream is about disenchantment and love.

Here is the dream: I am on a panel that is judging a contest for the World Trade Center memorial about half a year after September 11th. I am furious with the entries. They all seem to follow a similar line of thought—to contrast male aggression with a soft feminine nature. "This is a stupid dichotomy!" I grow irate. "What then would you propose?" I am asked, "it is easy to criticize."

I find a memorial. Or I made it myself. I don't know which. I remember not knowing in the dream. It is a wall of concrete and entangled in the concrete are angel's trumpets: twisted, bent, mutilated by the concrete encasing. Hundreds upon hundreds of them. It brings to mind the remains of the World Trade Center. I say to them, "nothing can be said and nothing can be heard." Nothing. It is a memorial to impotence.

Angel's trumpets? They were given trumpets after the last seal was opened during the revelations. It is a time of enforced silence. The silence signaled that God was moving into action. The angels were to be his emissaries. The sounds on their trumpets would signal his bidding—his judgment upon humanity. With each sound of the trumpet a different woe upon humanity. Destruction of what is provides for the impending birth of a new era. The trumpets were this apocalyptic comingling of life and death. St. Paul says: "For the trumpet will sound, and the dead will be raised imperishable, and we will be changed. For this perishable body must put on imperishability, and this mortal body must put on immortality" (1 Cor. 15:51–53). The work of angels—it is said that they have never experienced death. Mortals, marked by death, need them. We need salvation. They announce the possibility of resurrection. Angels are also, one might remember, unsexed.

So what then of my encasing of their trumpets? No more life and no more death. No more destruction and no more creation. Nothing. What is the wish? It is a wish precisely for this nothing. Nothing said, nothing heard, nothing done, nothing new. The landscape is barren. I told you. I'm still grinning.

It is difficult for me to understand what it means to wish for such a thing. "It is not quite remembering is it," was said to me at the time.

I disagreed. This is my memory. I have very little, but this is what I know. I am close to Adorno's attachment to impotence, his Eros of castration. The memorial felt familiar, like home. The tortured memorial was a comfort. This feeling permeated the dream. No more exile. No more fatigue. This is *it*—the emphasis on the last syllable showing the longing for death.

You cannot speak and you cannot hear. This judgment was leveled at everyone, including of course my analyst. No false utopia. No maternal idolatry. No denunciation of all things male. It is a stupid dichotomy. I still agree. But there is something stupider about a memorial to nothing, said with a kind of retaliation. What kind of nothing? It is a nothing that is given substance. Contrasted with the emptiness of the vase, it is the subtle difference between impotence and impossibility.

I was the authority in this dream. The monument commanded my authority. I told you so. Adorno is always right. His arguments were constructed that way. The future anterior here in the guise of pedagogy has the force of stasis. This is not its meaning. If there is any truth in this dream it is that the memorial is not real however much I wished it to be so. If we can give up the demand for the essential relation, we can say nonidentity without it actually having to be so. The truth of the dream is an impossibility I wasn't yet able to recognize.

For Lacan, this is the irremediable divide between signifier and the thing (signified), between a signifier and the emptiness or absence on which it is founded. It is this reaching suspension concretized that is imaged by the dream. "Man fashions this signifier and introduces it into the world in the image of the Thing whereas the problem is the Thing is characterized by the fact that it is impossible for us to imagine it. Here is the problem of sublimation" (Lacan, 1973/1981, p. 114). As with any creation, sublimation is, like the vase, molded around an inner emptiness, marked by the absence of the Thing that cannot be written, resists imagination. To attempt to give this real its place, its locus, is the impossible act that this dream turns around.

That wasn't how I wanted it. One can always hold onto an object in melancholia. What I felt after the dream was hardly a compassion for the wish to be heard or the desire to speak, but a sense of outrage, perhaps sadness. The punitive voice—*what would you propose, it's all so stupid, awful*—becomes a concrete wall hundreds of stories tall.

Looking at the two dreams, the inner emptiness of the vase is close to the void of the two towers and nothing heard or said in the *dream of the memorial*. In relation to this emptiness, we find in one the appearance of the letter, and in the other, the building of a memorial. The trumpets, their immanent judgment, my own, seems to transform—from the first dream to the second—into an imagined inheritance that is closer to home, but feels less so, in other words, more uncanny. This inheritance has its certainty, but it is tempered by this. *It is* becomes *it was, it will be,* or even, *it could have been*. Between the first and the second I think one can see that there was a great deal of work.

This was also evident in the feelings I could have about the dream. I could, for example, recognize the falsity of the letter. That letter was not my history, nor my memory. I could see the wish almost immediately and this recognition allows one to ask a question about desire. One turns to the image and asks a question about it. Why the vase in an attic? My arm reaching in, looking, I want to be a psychoanalyst. Perhaps I want to be a psychoanalyst with too much haste.

Here, with this dream of the memorial, at the time it was dreamt, there was something so compelling about it. Too compelling: a kind of fascinated paralysis. I didn't want to say anything. The declaration was made—*no one can*. The dream sets out to negate—no one can speak any longer, so no one will. My words are the last. Perhaps we might add that at the time of this dream, I, like Adorno, felt that words were not enough.

So the capacity to speak, even if in protest, even if it declares a kind of nothing, would be something else. For Lacan, speech is a happening. "It is not a happening that overflies, it is not a moment of knowing" (Lacan, 1975/1998, p. 38). It is something that has effects. We are in the business of a talking cure. One must believe that there is at least one who can hear. Transference love is this *one who can hear* consolidated in the figure of the analyst. It is one of the only reasons that patients continue—something must be heard, they believe in this listening ear.

In the dream of *the memorial* the said nothingness is tied too closely to the void created by the fallen towers. It relishes the void, eroticizes it even. The dream takes place in a mode of almost total negation, which, while a foundational truth in the psychoanalytic theory of mind, does not for all that end there. The dream takes negation and elevates it, literally. Not a cornerstone, but brick and mortar.

The truth of the work of angels is that *it is* a miracle that we can say anything at all. The experience in analysis gives this to us. The rage of the act of total negation is a testament to this precariousness. I am still trying to learn how to listen. How did Adorno put it? With a speculative ear. For my part, this is also the bearing out of disenchantment *and* the possibility of love. I misunderstood the dream at first. By the time of the second dream, I would no longer.

So the misinterpretation takes place in demanding a position outside or beyond impossibility. To undo the negativity at the heart of man, to erase the divide between the sexes—the outrage at the stupid dichotomy—is an impossible wish. The terrifying asymmetry of the law of their absolute difference points to the presence of the void. Certainly it is one truth, as Freud well knew, that we will spend a lifetime trying to reconcile. Love is the counterpart to desire, but the tunnel must be driven through from both ends, as he says in the *Three Essays* (1905b).

In an essay called *What is Love* (2000), Badiou asks about the relation between love, sex, gender, and philosophy. Far from philosophy being a willing denial of sexual difference, he makes the claim that philosophy has always addressed the obscurity of sex and sexual difference through the category of love. Love for Badiou is about the encounter of the two with the fact of their eternal separation. No theme, perhaps contrary to appearances, requires more pure logic. "It is thus necessary to keep the pathos of passion, error, jealousy, sex, and death at a distance" (Badiou, 2000, p. 266).

Love, Badiou says, gives us over to the thought of the two, to the absolute disjunction between two positions. This is what it acknowledges or names in the loving encounter. The words *I love you* bring into relation two pronouns, I and you, that were originally disjunct and always threaten to return there once again. Even further, "the experience of the loving subject … does not constitute a knowledge of love. This is even a distinctive feature … the thought that it is, is not the thought of its thought. Love, as an experience of thought, does not think itself" (Badiou, 2000, p. 266). The disjunction then is not only between one person and another, but between experience and thought, between love and knowledge. This aspect of love must be preserved. It cannot slip into the *pathos* of love conceived as fusional (making One), ablative (what he'll call the prostration of the same on the alter of the Other), pessimistic (i.e., love as a fundamentally illusory cover for the horror of sexual difference), or legal (i.e. love as a contractual relationship, such as marriage).

For Badiou, the thought of absolute disjunction and love is perhaps just another name for Being and the Event. He locates a series: one, two, infinity. In love, the two fractures the one and tests the concept of infinity. It shows that there is ultimately no third position except that which names this encounter with the void. This is what lovers in loving are faithful to, namely the event of their love. It is an idea of love as fidelity to an experience—one that tries to escape the traps of romanticism, the coldness of utilitarian notions of love, and the solipsism of a skeptical pornographic eye.

Love cuts through one's habitual ways of being that cover over the abyss that divides and opposes us. Somehow, through this other that I love, I allow myself to forcefully encounter this gap. This is not a third position. It is an event that marks the inability for there to be a third that sutures the two once and for all. Badiou calls this long sought after third, the angel, and he prohibits it—"it engages an imaginary function" (Badiou, 2000, p. 267):

> The discussion regarding the sex of angels is so important because its stakes are to pronounce on the disjunction. But this cannot be done from the point of experience alone .... What is it, then, which makes it possible for me, here, to pronounce on the disjunction without recourse to, or without fabricating, an angel? Since the situation alone is insufficient, it requires supplementation. Not by a third structural position, but by a singular event (Badiou, 2000, p. 267).

No angels, no third, only disjunction and event. This is Badiou's logically purified philosophical version of love, an attempt to shorn love of an unrelenting pathos that haunts it.

As was noted, Freud (1914) in *On Narcissism* says that loving as opposed to being loved forces one to tolerate a depletion in this opening of the self onto the other. Or, as Lacan puts it:

> I suggest that there is a radical distinction between loving oneself through the other—which, in the narcissistic field of the object, allows no transcendence to the object included—and the circularity of the drive, in which the heterogeneity of the movement out and back shows a gap in its interval (Lacan, 1973/1981, p. 194).

It is this movement generated by loving that mirrors the pathway of all events: What can one know of the beloved? How does one remain faithful? Why are faith and betrayal the stakes of this act? Why does love always threaten to collapse back into the oblivion of solitude? Love happens, that we know, but its difficulty, the ways of maintaining its life or leaving it to death, are a continued site of thought. For Badiou this thought is only possible if impossibility refuses to beckon after angels.

That the third, thirdness, or triangulation, has been floating in the psychoanalytic and philosophical ether for some time now, despite its present vogue, amuses me given this outright prohibition by Badiou. How can thought not engage this "imaginary function" of the angel? How is thought drawn by something as precarious as love or Eros? For Lacan, surely it is to begin with his permanent and absolute negation—there is no sexual relation. Love is to give what one does not have. Adorno's negativity, the impossibility of a true life in the false one, echoes as a similar kind of starting point.

Is this not a starting point for all ethical questions, questions that stand at the beginning of psychoanalysis, its cure? Placing at the fore-front problems concerning ethical life forces one to begin with its negative possibility, the fact that it has not been realized. History is this constraint, that failure. While this may be a given for Lacanians (intrinsic to the way they read Freud), even for most critical theorists or philosophers who begin with reading Hegel in the negative, it does not seem to be the route traveled by the psychoanalysts.

Does an underlying positivism inevitably put psychoanalysis on a different track than the one beginning to be outlined here? Is this angel the current function of any ideal of mental "health" regardless of one's model of the psyche? Does psychoanalysis, whenever it forms an idea of its end, inevitably fall into the traps of an ideal? I wish it were not so.

For Freud, the desire inherent in love and work can only be understood through its own mythic origin—the killing of the father, a first desire to possess one's mate, women entering into an economy of exchange, humans banding together in small communities, acceptance of a prob-lematic division of labor, establishment of guilt and law—namely what Lacan calls the humanization of sexuality. Failure is always first *this* failure. The failure is the failure of civilization and the attempt to trans-form or translate desire into a stable communal structure.

It is, as Freud has shown, always predicated on an impossible equi-librium between possession of the good/expulsion of the bad. The universal failure of neurosis, our enduring discontent, is the failure of the relation between desire and these sedimented repressions of culture. Extending backward, we find a mythical past where man was first and forever divided from nature.

Love and work are almost for Freud equal in necessity as failure. Sublimation is the most narrow and impossible of solutions, itself coming at a great cost to the satisfaction of the drive. The prolonged period of infantile helplessness, *Hilflosigkeit*, the diphasic nature of sexuality, the strangulating effects of the family, and the subsequent personalization of disappointment in the realm of human relations, colored sadomasochistically, is our lot. Psychoanalysis begins here and the solutions it provides, the so-called cure, is unknown. It is what is not yet—what is to come by the work of analysis alone. Perhaps it is a contribution to a culture where, as Freud says, *every man must find out for himself in what particular fashion he can be saved* (see, Freud 1930). No positive conclusions should be sought. Theoretically psychoanalysis is descriptive not proscriptive.

Any good in an analysis that is not the patient's own, or even further, one that does not spring directly from the passions of the symptom, is therefore, for Lacan, an imaginary function. We have psychoanalysis and we have orthopedic therapeutics. The disagreement about essentialism behind this split is so fundamental it practically seems irresolvable.

For now, I would have to admit that this is painfully true, particularly to the extent that essentialism is read by Lacanians to be at the heart of the neurotic conflict with respect to mastery. The neurotic demand is always a demand for an essential relation—be it one of love, knowledge, or the place that the two intersect. If psychoanalysis takes up a position that deems this possible or even merely positive, even theoretically, then it cannot submit a neurotic demand to analysis, at least not in good faith.

If Adorno was where I began, it has taken me quite some time to understand, which is to say to overcome a blinding disappointment, that this is not the case for a great deal of the field encompassed by the words psychoanalytic. Oddly, if this was a feat in its own right, it took moving closer to Lacan, understanding his way out of this depth of negativity, to know this. This was to know what Adorno meant for me in particular, so that I could situate his difference within a field of general meanings.

So the strange conceit of this work is that it starts in a place whose premise is perhaps untenable for almost all but the converted for whom it was not written. Since it seeks neither to persuade nor convert in itself, I have to ask, has it been written for no one at all. Allow me perhaps to console myself by believing that at the very least in not being written for anyone, it certainly doesn't ask to be sent an angel. One virtue is enough.

LACAN

With an eye for the one who is vanishing

Beginning with Lacan is one of the hardest things to do. That his discourse even brings into question what it might truly mean to begin, which means that a whole lot of us never do, makes it all the more difficult because one starts to question themselves which is to go in the wrong direction entirely because in questioning oneself one is caught in an act of reflection that will never be an act in the proper sense of carving out a beginning. It is, in effect, just one more inhibition. In fact it may be inhibition *par excellence*. And if I'm already involving you in a dizzying set of logistics it is hopefully not for no reason; but certainly if one follows Lacan, the *not for no reason* is already quite suspect. With the double negation, perhaps all we can do is hope that we arrive at something a little bit more than not.

So it is with Lacan that one is trapped between a something that always amounts to nothing, his definition of the object, and a nothing that nevertheless must be made something, his hopes for the subject. About this, what does one say? Well, Lacan did that for the twenty-eight years of his seminar. And maybe then ask, what does one write? Well, Lacan surely did not do that, but, if I am not to be just one more contribution to the secondary elaboration of discourse, one that he never meant to be, then I don't see anything other than the necessity for some extraordinary sacrifice. Those who take up the position of knowledge do so with an eye for the one who is vanishing—to reassure themselves that they are, not them, not there, with their gaze fixed on the horizon.

My part, I think it shall be lost. It is in its way a very feminine solution, which is a fine way to begin since the one thing I do know about Lacan is that he loved women. Through Lacan I will take up what Adorno left behind—the question of what form of sacrifice is necessary and what about this question is specifically feminine. Let us return to mythic origins.

A child stares at the television watching a nature show much like any other—the social behavior of a pride of lions. One scene in particular will be remembered. There is some determination at work. What would pique this child's curiosity, narrow the attentional field, and open into excitement seems preordained. The father of the pride exiles himself. There can only be one and he is now too old to hold his place. From this moment on he will wander the plains in solitude. His work is done. He leaves without looking back. Sons were exiled from the pride once they reached puberty. There could only be one father so they lived alone or in the company of others awaiting their chance to take a pride for themselves. The anxious wait is over. Now was their moment.

The child, for a second, finds the space to wonder—how was this day chosen? By whom was it chosen? The new male enters the scene. One by one he slaughters the children of the old rival, announcing his arrival and dominion. Another question appears. Why? The other isn't a threat having left willingly? Before an answer is found the females go instantly into heat. Head to neck they nuzzle him. It marks a turn, a new generation.

One sees much as a child and remembers little. For this child, this memory held. It is certainly a screen, but a screen for what, we might ask? What could its everyday, dare I say *natural*, ordinariness screen? Surely, analytically, we would begin to speculate. Primal scene. Indeed! Mothers are whores. Fathers are impotent or virile. Children are excluded, betrayed, and sacrificed. Can anything else be said?

This interpretation is hardly commensurate with the picture of a child's eyes laying claim to these images. All the keys to sexuality, its crucial nexus in the subject, are contained herein, not as deterministic, but as a location mapped between a series of events:

> The mode in which a work touches us, touches us precisely in the most profound fashion, namely on the unconscious plane, has to do with an arrangement, a composition of the work which no doubt ensures that we are interested very precisely at the level of the unconscious; but this is not because of the presence of something which really supports before us an unconscious (Lacan, 1958, L18.3.59, p. 4).

This is not *simply* an infantile or unconscious fantasy. It has something to do with logic, with an arrangement that interests us on the level of the unconscious. In one instantaneous glance the constraints imposed upon our very being are captured in a series of transactions that unfold.

We have to follow the structure in the series of displacements. The intrusion of the unfolding sequence short-circuits the questions that arise. The father? The children have been killed. The dead child? The mother is in heat. The father, who had left of his own accord, appears as someone who has been murderously eclipsed and betrayed. It gives the impetus for his murder to be avenged; the death wish resurrected and justified as a point of pride.

What this obscures is the fact that the father's place exists *only* because of its potential absence, that its nature is symbolic in value. The father isn't identifiable with the presence of this father or that father who attempts to substitute for him—the father is a placeholder, a name. The child captures this, wondering about an anonymous force (*how was this day chosen … but he left willingly*), a structure that holds beyond the participants at hand. The father's potential, perhaps inevitable, sacrifice of his place is the condition of its possibility. He recognizes it as something beyond his self-presence. His failing preserves the function that he demarcates.

This minimal difference granted to the father, between himself and his place, is one saving grace—and certainly it is one that saves. The death wish does not proliferate in his name, but his name serves as a marker that runs counter to the wish. Accepting this means one must accept him, and perhaps oneself also, as substitutable and displaced. To this child perhaps it is not yet possible. The recognition is there, but it quickly disappears.

In Oedipus something must be renounced, sacrificed, in the name of a future guarantee. Sacrifice shifts in the drama of Sophocles from the act of infanticide, to murder, usurpation, and finally, self-castration. Sacrifice brings into play an unfolding sequence in the gap between the generations and the sexes, and only at the extreme end, in a moment of self-dissolution, does it locate the limit. If sacrifice has something to do with establishing one's particular identity, it is a story that inevitably goes awry. But, it does so in particular ways, ways that are bound to a particular set of constraints.

Here, what goes awry can be seen in the act of remembering. To understand this, we have to proceed backward like most analyses of symptoms that take place in two moments, separated by a gap. There is something that is primary (yes also primal perhaps) in so far as it is *before* the excitement generated in the virile identification with the ravaging father, the ravished child, and the insatiable woman. This primary moment and its secondary effects points to a disjunction in a field of absence and presence, silence and the fury of fantasy. Something turns around an object and its absence. Sacrifice is not only a site where aggression, guilt, and punishment rear their head as obscene vicissitudes of the death drive. What we can also see is that there is a structure that it begins to highlight. The child, we might say, is looking for a way to give something up.

When Lacan returned to the question of hysteria, in particular through the Dora case, he read the case backward to understand the place her father held for her. It is the father whose origin and destiny as failure envelops the case and no doubt the repetition in the transference. Dora is on the scent of the father's relation to sacrifice. In life he sacrifices her, in her first dream he refuses to—"I refuse to let myself and my two children be burnt for the sake of your jewelcase" (Freud, 1905b, p. 64). He is the powerful, saving father. In the second dream, Dora has perhaps found a way to sacrifice him—certainly a moment of revenge, the death wish—but also something more than just that.

It is this more that Freud admittedly failed to pick up … the *jewelcase*, the nymphs, Frau K's adorable white body, the Sistine Madonna. These hold the final word on her desire and point to the nodal organizers in the dream: representations, pictures, a geography of sexuality, a map of femininity. We can only imagine that Freud, having been able to mark this desire, could have found a different end than her morbid craving for revenge. She could have found a way to give way on her pride.

The structure of this failed father in relation to the feminine is a structure, Lacan says, that psychoanalysis has completely forgotten about, having become absorbed in the secondary elaboration of a virile fantasy. In fact, Lacan calls the myth of the strong Oedipal father Freud's hysterical symptom. Even in the sadomasochistically rendered scene between the mother and child—which the father, not failing, successfully interrupts—psychoanalysis repeats the fantasy. It was evident to Lacan that this question was also the question Freud (1939) struggled with at the end of his life with the two Moses, or even before with his question about matriarchy and the primal horde in *Totem and Taboo* (1912–1913).

There must be a beyond to the demand for the benevolent unmovable virile father who is equal to himself. Sacrifice read from within a posthaste arrangement cannot conceive of a beyond, is riveted to the spot. The logic has more to say about what couldn't be said, coming to be occupied by these imaginarized scenes. The child's attention was already drawn to the place of absence itself; drawn to this marker of difference and disjunction. However, this gap is quickly filled. Pride above all else seems to demand it. Children, when I think of them, are creatures of pride out of necessity. Pride then must eventually give when this necessity falls away.

Moving on. A child is told the story of *The Little Mermaid* by Hans Christian Anderson (1836/1992). She's the father's favorite. Her voice is one of the most coveted objects in all the seas so it is her voice that she will lose. Like so many figures in fairytales, she is, for some reason or another, mute. In fact, for this princess, it is without her voice that she must win the heart of a man. Sacrifice of this precious object is the price of her reaching for any beyond, in particular anything beyond the constraints of her family. She fixes her eyes on the furthest horizon—to be loved by a human and to be given immortality in an afterlife with mortals and god.

"Pride must suffer pain," she was told by her paternal grandmother—it is the condition of becoming a woman. From beginning to end, nothing is gained in this story without a cost. When she comes of age and can visit the surface of the sea, she is painfully adorned with oyster shells. Whenever she dances, a vision of absolute grace, each step cuts into her like a thousand blades. She not only has to seduce the impossible, she must seduce with impossibility. The thought of death, it is said, weighs heavily on her heart. She silently endures it.

In the end, the prince marries another woman that he misrecognizes as her. The mermaid princess is condemned to death. She cannot tell him of the pain of losing his love nor the very mistake that he has made. Yet, it is not clear that she would have told him even if she could. Given one last chance to live by her sisters, shorn of their beautiful hair, she can kill her prince with a magic knife and return home. She will not do it. She chooses her fate—her heart shatters and she is dissolved into foam upon the waves. Admiring the courage of the little mermaid, the daughters of the air offered her a place with them in their work circulating the winds on the surface of the earth.

Destiny hangs on the power of another. We are subjected to this Other. Love for this prince in the case of *The Little Mermaid*, but even more than this, her history. The words that come from her paternal line—her father and her father's mother—seem to determine her path. They deliver her to her fate in the form of a life of pain that is to be commensurate with her sexual desire. For pride, she must suffer. Sexuality and death move hand in hand.

The Oedipal interpretation: this is the bind of being an Oedipal winner. You force the loss of what was most coveted in you. As punishment? Perhaps. You should not have enjoyed that. Fathers should not be so seductive. Renunciation is a moral lesson on how to live happily. The princess does not heed this lesson. "The prince's happiness is my happiness", she willfully declares. She desires only, and pathologically, through him.

But a question opens up: Has she repressed her incestuous desire too much or not enough? Must she temper her desire, a desire always bound at the extreme end of a wager, at the cost of her life? Or has she, in fact, renounced her desire to be the chosen one, faithful instead to a desire that goes beyond being only the beloved? Misrecognition of this desire seems to rule the day. She leaves in her wake the enigma of woman's love. It is somehow *both* a terrifying excess and the heights of renunciation.

We can see in *The Little Mermaid* her attempt to find her desire, to find it in love always subject to the hazards of chance. She is faithful. Otherwise *it is* a very boring and moralistic tale. Love, bound up with death at the most extreme point of passage, indeed in suicide, is a confrontation with fate and necessity—a formal rendering of desire. The little mermaid must try and pass through a certain threshold.

Is this not allegorized by her transformation into a daughter of the air? Through her sacrifice, she regains her life once again which takes on an exigent character. Life becomes driven. I will have to insist that these stories, their constellations, expose the impasse of an encounter between the sexes and the generations. This tale turns on the mermaid princess having to test the limits of love, of what one would be willing to do and endure for the sake of love, inverting the message that is handed down to her. If pride must suffer pain, that pain must become a pain unto death, a point of pride that is also the dissolution of pride.

There are always two women in these stories, the real love and her double. Life for this man is always more comfortable with the double. In fact, that life is secured by the sacrifice of the other. This, as a fact about men, is of little consequence. That choice was necessary for her to make her final move. Faithful to her prince, she was able to mark the threshold of this beyond. Finding a means for the circulation of desire defines both a subjectivizing movement and the play of femininity through various guises of sacrifice. These seem coupled through desire.

The little mermaid is one of those icons of femininity that no doubt feminists would rally against. A male fantasy of feminine self-sacrifice? Perhaps. I prefer to see how the limits of both the merman kingdom and the human world are overturned in act that rubs up against both through silence, grace, and determination. Through fidelity the beauty of the princess is made to appear in all its brilliance. This could be a tale of the errant man who fails to be captivated by such beauty, the inverse tale of the Siren's song. The mermaid cannot sing after all—such is her sacrifice and her wager.

Lacan, as we said, claimed that he speaks with no hope of being heard. Hearing, with no hope of speaking, I think somehow also puts things back into circulation. Speaking, making oneself heard, like loving or listening without an investment in a return, reaches out toward the Other. The real threat seems to be if this mermaid princess had succeeded in her masquerade—her pretty white legs a sought after phallic substitute. With this substitute, what becomes of desire and its interminable movements? If earlier we moved from sacrifice to virility, here we make the reverse move from virility to sacrifice.

A tale of adolescent impetuousness surely but love without impetuousness doesn't move. It seems to me that the story's end points to this question about fathers and the feminine—the little mermaid, in act of self-shattering, joins the daughters of the air in their quest to do good between the earth and the heavens above. Desire, aimed at this breaking point, finds a means of circulation. Has not our mermaid princess renounced every phallic value of having? The pretty white legs didn't stand a chance. Eternal life depends upon a power beyond us, the spirits of the air tell her. As her eyes fill with tears, she looked down and smiled upon her prince and his bride. She was happy, it was said. She had found another way of living.

The mermaid princess is one of many renditions of the tale of the passage of a virgin girl into womanhood. Let us turn to the next in the series, child, girl, woman, and mother. If the father as failure is one side of the polarity, the mother on the other end seems absolutely criminal. A vision of excess. She is a trespasser, a terrifying violator of the boundaries of hearth and home. The one who *would have* if it weren't for some limit that was held—perhaps by him, perhaps by others. One trembles before a mother or finds amnesty. Hers are the blows of fate like an unending potential for terrible violence.

One might imagine that this forms a lure in the image of a self-sacrificing daughter turned mother; that self-sacrifice, in the case of woman, must be made a necessary virtue. In fact, the desire to be a mother, the imputed narcissistic origin of such a wish, is a wish to be continually counteracted. Psychoanalysis has its own problematic version: the girl, deprived of her father, envious of his glorious appendage, acquiesces to a replacement in the form of receiving a baby from a father-substitute. Her painful destiny as not-male finds its fulfillment in her role as mother.

The solution, they say, is always too tenuous. Hysteria lingers around every corner, with every fresh disappointment. The psychoanalyst recoils: her super-ego is uneducable, she is prone to depression, and her claims are always too great. Is the baby or the husband the faltering substitute? Or do both, proving inadequate, need the supplement of the other? Motherhood also? She does not sublimate easily or well. It is not Kronos who devours his children, always mothers.

The little mermaid's life of renunciation seemed necessary. Much as there was something important to read beyond this, the manifest demand for a mother's sacrifice should be grasped in another fashion as well. Once again Nicole Loraux proves instructive. If the feminine as the object of appropriation or expulsion guided us through Greek tragedy, so too might the Athenian laws that surround the mothers—

in particular, the decree that mourning mothers be secluded in their homes. A mother's grief over the death of her child, her lamentation, is, like most incarnations of the feminine, a threat to the unity of the *polis*.

Her grief, they say, is too easily transformed into wrath. She is unable to sublimate this feminine grief for the needs of the city, notably a city that needs warriors. There is a utilitarian ethic at odds with personal pain. The singular and terrible tie between a mother and her child must be broken for the greater good. The examples multiply: Hecuba, Jocasta, Eurydice, Clytaemnestra, and Antigone.

Mourning and femininity seem inextricably linked and mourning is itself depicted as feminizing. Achilles is told that his grief over Patroklus is unmanly, which is repeated by Shakespeare in words from Claudius to Hamlet in the opening familial scene. Loraux says, "a mother's sorrow is general in the sense that it is generic, a general sorrow that contains all mourning within it. A mother has given birth to mourning" (1988/1998, p. 3). This mourning to which she gives birth is emblematic of all mourning, all sadness.

Much as the body is exiled by Platonic philosophy, so too the mourning of a mother is negated in an imperative order by Athens that one forget. Athenians must swear an oath to the city not to remember *the misfortunes*. An alter to Lethe, oblivion, is erected deep in the Erechtheion on the Acropolis, enjoining us under the banner of repression.

Electra is perhaps the exemplary figure of this *pathos* of mourning and in her exemplary mourning she mirrors the mother that she loathes. Although saying little about his supposed Electra complex, Freud must have gleaned this mode of refusal from her tale. Electra cannot mourn the loss of her father, killed by her mother Clytaemnestra as retribution for his killing their daughter, Electra's sister, Iphigenia. Perhaps Electra wishes it were she who was the chosen object of sacrifice, the cause. Certainly thereafter it is the sacrifice of her grief that she will not make. The affirmative oblivion of the utilitarian law of Athens meets here with Electra's nonoblivion—her refusal to forget that consumes her alone.

Both processes, Loraux points out, are essentially a temporal. We move from negation—I will not recall—to Electra's constant language of double negation—never to be veiled, never to be undone, never to be forgotten. Forgetting is linked to forgiveness and amnesty through a question of memory. Where does this utilitarian law of forgetting begin and end? And who would dare obliterate for good the unique memory of the beloved? These stories about mothers bring to the surface an order centered on questions of love and memory.

Many of the plays, Antigone perhaps best, show the virtues of an ethic of desire that refuses in the face of all laws to give up this loving tie to the object. If it ceases, so will she in the form of death—she declares in her grief. What is sublime in tragedy is precisely this devotion. It seems to me that the difference that separates Electra from a figure like Antigone cannot be located through any question of their excess. It is rather a question about movement, time, circulation, and the work of mourning which gathers (not expels) the desire of these women.

Electra, to the extent that one might fault her, is trapped in the double negation—she cannot and does not act. She is a figure who waits. Electra makes no appeal and forgives no one. Her double negation is a statement, a testament to her own static, self-identical willing. Antigone, Clytaemnestra even, are figures for whom mourning poses a problem and that problem means that an appeal must be made at all costs—Antigone to a higher divine order, Clytaemnestra to justice through the furies. They make themselves heard, the appeal forces the city to respond, obviating a disjunction between the Law and individual desire. Amnesty is neither obvious nor possible without a kind of work.

A way of continuing seems to me to be what is crucial in each of these stories, even with Electra who can find a way to continue only by continuing to mourn. It is rather well worn knowledge that exchange, debt, renunciation, guilt, and sacrifice, form an Oedipal constellation around desire and prohibition. But like the Athenians, we too dream of alleviation from these constraints, constraints that are perhaps bedrock. Alleviation then would have to be alleviation from the conflict between generations, an excess in sexuality, the problems of subjection to the caprice of others, the bind of grief and love. This desire, as Freud knew well, is the desire for death.

For psychoanalysis, one cannot be alleviated from these impossible constraints. One is responsible for finding a way. Forgetting or never forgetting, Athens and Electra, form a kind of illusory eternal order here on earth. Desire is something else than this. Suspended in a plea measured between earth and sky, these mothers beckon after an eternal order that is only ever beyond the world in which they immediately live. Their grief, their abjection, trembles on this limit.

Freud (1937) spoke of an original terror of passivity—the so-called bedrock of castration. In every solution within these stories there is a moment where the longstanding oppositions between passivity and activity, femininity and masculinity, and individual and community, find their appearance in and through a sacrificial act. That act does not cover over that opposition but finally makes it obvious, perhaps thereby prompting some way forward.

This solution can be read moralistically and condemned. It is a condemnation, in particular, that seems leveled at women and children. There is a curious correspondence between this moralism and the path of a virile identification. Sacrifice as a means of finding one's desire points to a logic other than this one, and, rather than taking up the virile position, reads backward from it. I would at least expect that analysts would begin to pick up from this very point and point not to alleviation, condemnation, or identification (which, in this case, is only imagined virility), but something else.

This something else is indeed what Freud tried to construct with his notion of the *bedrock of castration* and its relationship with sublimation. If it is bedrock, where else have we to go? The act is both a fall, rock bottom, and the heights to which perhaps only then we may rise, the dignity of sublimation. There is, regardless of one's anatomical sex, something like a bedrock refusal of castration, a repudiation of femininity (Freud, 1937). The cure only follows from a gratitude for what one never wants to sacrifice.

One more story. Anna O., the first analysand, became fond of a parable she found written by a woman in her family history in her maternal line:

> During a storm, a nest of young birds was at risk from flooding. Papa bird brought his little ones to safety, one by one. While flying above the teeming flood with the first of his young, carefully held in his claws, he asked, "look at the amount of trouble I am going through in order to save you; will you do the same for me when I am old and weak?"—"Of course I will," the first replied. At which the father promptly dropped him in the water, with the words, "one should not save a liar." The same went for number two. When asking the question of the third and last one, he received the following answer: "My beloved father, I cannot promise you that; but I do

promise that I will save my own little ones." The papa bird saved
this young one (Verhaeghe, 1999, p. 170).

Anna O., had nursed her father for years, found in this parable a father
who could save his brood only in finding through them a way not to
need to be saved himself. Furthermore, the *declaration* of sacrifice makes
you a liar. Anna O.'s first analyst, as we know, like the prince of the
mermaid princess, withdrew from the scene in the face of her desire.

This story painfully echoes Anna O.'s real-life fate. In one of her last
poems she laments that "love had passed her by," and indeed it seems
that she never had a loving sexual relationship. The little bird tries to
find a way not to sacrifice her desire for that of her father. Yet, what
remains seems only to be the negativity of the wish—*not to for him*—
rather than desire in its own right. Like the father bird, Anna O. cannot
put into question why she questions her children as she does.

Love, in the fashion of King Lear, was an impossible submission and
her desire for a *true* sacrifice was only realized by the sacrifice of any
and all love objects. It reads as a rather uncanny repetition of the story
that unfolds in *Studies in Hysteria (1895d)*. Only able to reverse the order
of power, close to her death, it was reported that she said, "if there is
any justice in the next life, women will make the laws there and men
will bear the children" (cited in, Britton, 1999, p. 3).

So this *will-to-sacrifice* did not occur as a transformation in her subjective position. This means of sacrifice did not prove a means of transforming desire beyond a commitment to a desire for dissatisfaction.
As Lacan says of altruism:

> The altruism of the neurotic, contrary to what one says, is perma-
> nent. And there is no more common path to the satisfactions he is
> seeking than what one can describe as devoting oneself to satisfy-
> ing, as far as one can for the other, all the demands, which he well
> knows, however, constitute in his case a perpetual failure of desire
> or, in other words: to blind oneself in one's devotion to the other
> one's own dissatisfaction (Lacan, 1958, L03.6.59, p. 403).

In Anna O's repeated attempts to articulate her position—through her
many stories, poems, and plays, in her admirable social work—one
can see this difficult, but ultimately untaken step, clearly within sight.

With an ironic, sharp tongue, Lacan declares that this common path is a permanent one—permanent dissatisfaction, permanent blindness to one's own desire, in other words, the permanent *jouissance* of the moral masochist.

So the difference between the little mermaid and these mothers in suffering from the figure of Anna O. (and we must qualify the difference between a life and a work of fiction), is the denouement. They disappear, vanish, while their desire remains. Death is a kind of metaphorical passage for the sacrifice entailed in any transformation—putting into relief this bedrock as our vanishing point. Desire seems to require it.

In *Tragic Ways of Killing a Woman* (1985/1987), Nicole Loraux demonstrates the tie between disappearance, concealment, femininity, and desire, through the deaths of women in Greek tragedy. These deaths follow a precise logic for they are only staged in certain ways and very particular words are used. Women, as we've noted before, are hanged, whereas men die by the sword. Hanging contains a very clear idea of movement. It is elevation, flight, rising up, as well as throwing oneself down, falling into the depths: "the same word, *aiero*, which means elevation and suspension, applies to these two flights in opposite directions, upwards and downwards, as though height has its own depth: as though the place below, whether that be the ground or the world under that, could be reached only by first rising up" (Loraux, 1985/1987, p. 18). For Loraux, a woman's death must always signify movement, and the more feminine the figure the more the emphasis lies on this—reaching its pinnacle in the flight of a bird that makes its escape.

Silence is another adornment of women in tragedy, the maintenance of silence under threat, accusation, and, censure. They can and will conceal their desire. This is linked to the bodily sight of death chosen for women. Through hanging, strangulation, slitting their neck, it is aimed at the throat. Women tear at their throats in moments of extreme grief. The throat, Loraux shows, is connected to both voice and the breath:

> In the gynecological thinking of the Greeks, one is caught between two mouths, two necks, where vagaries of the womb suddenly choke the voice in a woman's throat, and where many a young girl old enough to be a nymphe hangs herself to escape the threat of the terrifying suffocation inside her body. Anyone at all familiar with Freud's work will remember Dora, the cough that was one of her symptoms, and the remarks of Freud on this "displacement

from the lower to the upper part of the body" which invade the throat because "that part of the body had to a high degree retained its significance as an erogenous zone in the young girl" (Loraux, 1985/1987, p. 34).

Loraux cautions the exaggerated use of this gynecological psycho-analytic baggage. Tragedy, she says, ultimately remains silent on such issues; the only place given firm allocation is death itself. These women die evoking a link between their sex and their voice. If these have been refused to them, then perhaps in accepting death, they make them their own once again.

We might remember that Freud's oral-erotic interpretation attempted to link Dora's oral symptoms to his construction that she imagined her father undergoing fellatio with Frau K as the sexual method of choice for a man without means. Freud contended that symptoms—her bouts of silence, her cough—used displacement upward from genitals to mouth. Lacan pointed out a strange error, for cunnilingus is clearly the sexual method for impotent men, foregrounding Freud's countertrans-ference. He missed the importance of the figure of Frau K whose ador-able little white body captivated Dora as the mystery of femininity. This countertransference silenced Dora, or perhaps we might say, allowed her to keep silent on this dimension of her desire. It also allowed her to prematurely end her treatment.

Feminine deaths in tragedy are not only cloaked in silence, they are all unseen. Every female death takes place off stage. Loraux concludes that a woman's tragic death is the only thing that belongs to her and the silence evokes this isolation. There are no words in a language of male renown that can give a place to a woman's death. While men's lives and deaths are written down in the history books—the glory of Athens—the woman remains a silent figure. These feminine deaths are bound by the secrets of body and home.

Keeping silent also meant that someone, at some point, was forced to speak of her, usually the chorus. What they come to say seems to center on the character of her will—her freedom, paradoxically, in the form of a submission to death. Through the act of refusal, which enve-lopes the tragic killing of a woman, the moment of choosing to submit is made conspicuous. This bivalent character of freedom and refusal, submission and silence, is particular to these feminine deaths and no others.

Loraux makes much of the sacrifice of the virgin Polyxena who, after struggling, bares her breasts to her sacrificer. It is both an act of defiance and acceptance that awes even her murderer:

> Greeks! You who razed my city!
> It is my will to die. Let no one touch my skin!
> I shall offer my throat in good courage.
> But let me stand free—I would die free!—for god's sake
> While you kill me.
>
> ...
>
> When she heard the command she took her robe at the shoulderpoint
> And tore it all the way to the navel.
> Exposed her breasts beautiful as a statue.
> Set her knee on the ground and spoke to all a word of absolute nerve:
> "Here! If you want to strike the chest, young man strike!
> Or, if you want the neck, I turn my throat to you!"
> And he, pitying the girl, cuts her breath in two."
> (Euripides, 2006, p. 124)

A woman must die free, or, rather, it is through death that we glimpse something of the freedom of desire.

I am reminded of Goethe's repugnance at Antigone's final lament in her tomb before her death. As Lacan (1986/1992) refers to it in the Ethics Seminar, "It's important that some madness always strike the wisest of discourses, and Goethe cannot help emitting a wish. 'I wish,' he says, 'that one day some scholar will reveal to us that this passage is a later addition' (p. 255). Goethe wanted Antigone to remain more steadfast in her will. He thought that would have made her a better heroine. But for Loraux, as Lacan, it is not a question of heroism and these moments, repeated throughout Greek tragedy, reveal something beyond individual heroics.

This something more is closely tied to the body, to the very tension of desire. For Loraux, this seems to be what tragedy emphasizes or tries to give representation to. There must be a fall *and* a flight. She must struggle *and* go willingly. She submits to her fate only to refuse once again, and she refuses only to reinforce her choice a second time. This highlights not only the difficulty of that choice, but the choice as a choice, through the medium of repetition. This building, wrenching tension, is desire, an experience that must be tolerated at the most extreme limit of the self, at its vanishing point. Through this play of affirmation and negation, their death is the counterpart to an exalted, but other-worldly, freedom and equanimity whose basis is desire itself.

"Whatever freedom the tragic discourse of the Greeks offered to women, it did not allow them ultimately to transgress the frontier that divided and opposed the sexes" (Loraux, 1985/1987, p. 78). Liberty, and the powerful place held within it by constraint, is played out in the field of communal life, only there where all paths lead to death. The sacrifice of virgins whose bodies are too inviolate, hanging which evokes falling and flying up, the sacrifice of the mermaid's pretty white legs, a mother's grief and memory, all point to a sacrifice made in order to establish the true frontier that divides and opposes the sexes wherein desire may be brought to life. Loraux does not judge nor make essential these markers of death and sexuality as they appear in the various constellations, circling around femininity or masculinity. The point is to trace this life of desire.

Perhaps this animates a faith, a faith that there is a limit that may shelter a beyond where a viable "temperate relation of one sex to the other" exists. A faith that desire can be a "desire to obtain absolute difference," that this would serve as an opening in the field of love for a desire "outside the limits of the law, where alone it may live" (Lacan, 1973/1981, p. 276). This, Loraux says, abides by a certain logic: "that which you win you instantly lose" (Loraux, 1985/1987, p. 45). We have to wonder, or at least hope, that the reverse may also be possible. Such would be the "delusional" faith of feminine sacrifice.

Femininity, submission, limit, sacrifice, and castration, form a much-disputed series. Aware of the contradictions and problems, I'm willing for the time being to accept this constellation of terms until a new one emerges that isn't merely a reversal in the direction of virility. If one wants to argue that this only comes into play as the result of a phallocentric fantasy, then perhaps that argument participates in a fantasy itself, namely of enforced equality. My point isn't to diagnose fantasy, but to put fantasy to use, to play with it. What other way is there with desire?

In any case, the limit that was taken as the aim in the Greek tragedies was not equality but absolute difference. Only in pushing toward absolute difference, living through the disjunction that marks it (Lacan's "*il n'y a pas de rapport sexuel*") can one even begin to conceive of freedom, justice, or liberty. This takes place through a work with fantasy, not against it. In a fictional world where women die monotonously by the throat and men's whole bodies are subject to penetration by swords, what becomes clear is that what is being constructed is this demarcating limit. That limit is established only in these death scenes which reconcile for a moment the disjunction in obviating it.

The irreducible reality of the anatomical distinction between the sexes, what gives us this terrible constellation of terms in the first place, is the only saving grace. But that grace only comes through a sacrifice whose specter, for the time, is always death itself. It is as if it is barely possible in *this* world. That it is only at the point where we move between this world and another unknown that we can begin to conceive of something else.

There are three questions we are told by Freud that a child cannot master: the sexual relation, the vaginal orifice, and the inseminating role of semen. Sacrifice becomes the act through which a boundary is made to appear in a constellation of lovers, women, fathers, and the violent parameters of living and dying—symbolic life itself. Sacrifice is surely a symptom, but it is a symptom precisely of this necessity for symbolic life, for something to come in the place where there is nothing and mark that impossible absence. As Lacan puts it:

> For the subject the object appears, if I may put it this way, on the outside. The subject is no longer the object: he rejects it with all the force of his being and will not find it again until he sacrifices himself (Lacan et al., 1977, p. 23).

Clinically we know all too well a field of neurotic renunciation, the stringent position that nothing can be had or gained or won. This strategy in fact protects the object of one's tenderness against this greater sacrifice. Adorno was master in this alone, and in this he declared an end to symbols, poetry, and art, no less philosophy.

The figure of omnipotence is there when the object is one that cannot be brought into this kind of play and circulation. Under a utilitarian law, perversion demands not elaboration, but a state of absolute well-being. If one cannot sacrifice, one murders *ad infinitum*. Always on this side of the pleasure principle, it lives according to its law—everything that is good is me, everything that is bad is you. The neurotic bemoans his subjection, a contortionist against the demands of life, and dreams of becoming this perverse figure. This logic of neurosis reverses these quadrants—everything that is bad is me, everything that is good is you.

In either case, one the negative of the other, ravaging fathers and ravished children, they all pay a price. Psychoanalysis, in elevating a certain kind of sacrifice that must be made, attempts to bypass these temptations—cowardice, perversion—*in abiding by their very logic, drawing out this logic to its end*. Psychoanalysis searches out the limit in order to stay there, trembling, as Adorno said, between fate and freedom.

What do these stories have to say then? Nothing, insofar as none of what constitutes their center speaks. The quiet self-delegated exile of a father, the mute princess' suicide in the name of love, a mother's grief, and all of those women hanged. The moment of continuing is always one that will refuse what introduces a form of stasis. Every act speaks to a turn in the generations or between the sexes. What is most intimate and personal finds a point of externality whose point of passage refuses, at bottom, any supplement, be it one of historical meaning, sense, moral lessons, or interpretation. It stands as it is. It asks nothing more than to be allowed to continue. What is new exists outside of sense, or between sense and nonsense, between what exists and what insists beyond existence. It *ex-sists*, or, as Lacan (2001) terms it, is *ab-sense*.

What do women know?

A whole movement of women began writing as a result of an encounter with Lacan's thought. The strange transaction that seems to take place isn't one of received wisdom, of mastering a body of knowledge, but something else, something that I would say is closer to wisdom about the body as that which fails in a particular way—fails in particular because of sexuality. The ego is first and foremost a necessary failure, namely a body ego. Despite the war between Lacan and so-called ego-psychology, it was to the question of the ego that he turned in his last seminars before his death, a question that I think cannot be dissociated from this question about the feminine to which he had also turned.

Lacan, in speaking about the fantasy Freud elaborated of watching a child being beaten, says that we should see in this something of an imaginarized scene that at bottom takes up the pain of life, our fall from grace—converting it into a scene of enjoyment. It is not only this scene, but the scene of the ego which must submit to the other agencies of the mind, one part turned around against the other. How do we accept the ways that we are subjugated and undone most intimately by the others that we love? Lacan says about it:

> you should recall that no matter how strange, how bizarre the phantasy of perverse desire may be in appearance, desire is always in some fashion involved in it, involved in a relation which is always linked to the pathetic, to the pain of existing as such, of purely existing, or of existing as a sexual term. It is obviously in this measure that the one who suffers injury in the sadistic fantasy is something which involves the subject in so far as he himself can be open to this injury, that the sadistic phantasy subsists … One cannot but be surprised that it has been thought possible to elude it for a single instant by making of the sadistic tendency something which in any way could be referred to a pure and simple primitive aggression (Lacan, 1958, L15.4.59, p. 9).

Perhaps here we can see the value of elaborating the so-called *feminine* position: passivity, submission, humiliation, abjection, the exit from one's own agency, the safety of voyeurism, and so on.

The problem for Lacan is always *jouissance*, not fantasy. The latter—in its relationship to desire—has an intimate bearing on the most universal of truths, even in its utterly perverse aspects. Gratification, *jouissance*, on the other hand, submerges truth along with desire, or one might say, submerges the truth of desire. Rather than constituting an opening, it may, in its isolation and repetition, become a point of closure.

Finding one's place in relation to another's writing poses similar difficulties: What opening can we find in their fantasy, what closes the other out? With Lacan, wanting to be gratified by him in the act of reading is instantly challenged. He meant it as much. I would say that after some time, I found in Lacan a kind of permission, an opening granted through the struggle with his work. Through him, I was able to accept more of what is impossible for me than through any other thinker, impossibility being something that a general hysteria usually converts to *jouissance*—the gratification of immediate refusal, outrage, or helplessness. Through him I was forced to find a certain kind of agency, and I was certainly forced to find my desire to continue reading.

Freud says in *Analysis Terminable and Interminable (1937)* that patient's come looking for a cure they do not want, namely this encounter with femininity. What patient's want an analyst to give them, something bearing the title of the phallus, cannot be given. Barring this, they will never allow themselves to be cured by another—they will not recognize a power beyond themselves. At the point where they might open themselves up to this beyond, they engage in intractable resistance. Analysis becomes interminable.

Termination seems to be dependant on the analysis creating the conditions for an encounter that gives it its end or limit. I think it is Lacan's recognition of this important *realm beyond the phallus* that appealed to so many women and created this desire to write. In Lacan's Encore Seminar (1975/1998), he speaks about love and *jouissance*. The confrontation with the impasse of the sexual relation, in particular with phallic *jouissance*, puts love to the test. Love must find some means of access to what lies beyond the phallus, which means that it has to confront this failure and impossibility. Lacan designates this realm femininity, or, for a less gendered variant, Other *jouissance*.

Analysis is a confrontation with this Other realm of possibility that he links with the act of writing. Analysis is "the displacement of the negation from the "stops not being written" to the "doesn't stop not being written", in other words, from contingency to necessity—there lies the point of suspension to which all love is attached" (Lacan, 1975/1998, p. 145). What doesn't stop not being written is everything that turns around absence in psychoanalysis—woman, fathers, authority, the sexual relationship, the unconscious. We encounter this absence and in doing so, make the negation shift—stops, doesn't stop, won't stop. We can see this in the move from Athenian *anēr*, to Electra and Antigone, from pride to the little mermaid's love and a mother's grief. What is important is to find a way to continue.

The problems of gratitude, and here I am quite in agreement with Melanie Klein, run deep. Love and gratitude are given by Lacan the sign of impossibility—they do not come without a tremendous struggle, they must be invented anew. Somehow, submitting to Lacan's work, finding pleasure in him, mirrored this impossible process of trying to make a negation, at many times a double negation, shift. To be grateful for what he was trying to do, for what he did, in particular, this act of teaching for twenty-eight years. The difficulty of Lacan, but even more so of having to follow his movements—from year to year in his seminars, from one joke to another, his shifts in register and conceptual system—required giving up, first and foremost, the idea that others understood what he was saying, perhaps above all, Lacan himself.

Ironically, Lacan calls out to the women in his audience on a number of occasions and asks them to say what it is that they know. He asks them to tell him about feminine sexuality and bemoans that they only keep silent. Lacan even seems to taunt them—if you aren't the worst analysts one might imagine that you would be the best, unsurpassable. But not a word.

In so many of these women writers, from Catherine Clément, to Michèle Montrelay, Luce Irigaray, Julia Kristeva, and others, it is not so much an answer in the form of divulging their secrets but a sheer act of writing that forms the response. Writing meets with voice, the last in a line of partial objects for Lacan, transformed by these women into a singular voice, perhaps feminine (it has been described as such), that informs both the form and the content of their works. It is as if saying something about the feminine can only be done as a feminine form of signature within an act of writing. Not a work on, but a work by, *this* woman.

Lacan (1975) will turn to this idea of signature as a final rendition of sublimation—a means of finding one's way with their unconscious and *jouissance*. He would like for desire, sublimated in this way, to take on a character much closer to the drive pure and simple—its rhythm and patterning. The important distinction Lacan makes at this late point, between his earlier theory that emphasized the symbolic and his late theory that focuses on the real, is that writing, being on the side of the latter, calls for no supplementation by meaning. It requires no third. Lacan is defining this dimension of the real in the signifier:

> What is this notion if we cannot define it as the very form into which desire flows ... or more exactly that the very notion of drive far from confusing itself with the substance of the sexual relation-ship, is this form itself, that it is the interplay of the signifier .... And it is also indeed as such that we can define sublimation. It is something through which, as I wrote somewhere, desire and the letter can become equivalent (Lacan, 1975, L 1.7.59, p. 433)

Unlike the elaboration of a symptom in psychoanalysis—the work of unraveling the network of signifiers—writing is closer to the formula of desire. It is closer to the formal qualities of unconscious desire: the very interplay, or play, of the signifier.

Patients come and they are certainly their particular selves. I do not intend to invoke the opposite register as one of diffusion, pathologizing as a vindication of identity—the Athenians were playing at that game long enough. If desire inhabits us as something that must remain alien, then it is not that the alien is gone once and for all at the end of analysis, a kind of anal fantasy. Where we stop cannot be a point of assimilation or imagined eradication. Lacan's play with this idea of signature is one way to talk about the end of an analysis—a singular mobilization of desire, a radical change in structure. This act of writing or signature is a way of putting to use a particular symptom rather than stagnating in the face of it.

I think the distinction between knowledge (*conaissance*) and know-how (*savoir-y-faire*) is important here. One does not understand desire—which in any case would be interminable—one finds a know-how through it. What analysis cultivates is one's unique signature that is both a way of being with desire and desires way of being. Signature and signifier become the formal play and act, not as a source of meaning, but a means of punctuation. Period. Exclamation. Semicolon. End. Lacan says in the *Les Non-Dupes Errent* seminar (1973), "one has to stop. One even asks for nothing but that" (L.13.11.73, p. 22). Meaning is endless.

The question of desire becomes central for Lacan in reinterpreting the importance of the limit and act of psychoanalysis. He discusses Freud's essay, *The Dissolution of the Oedipus Complex (1924)*, noting that if the child has to reconcile himself with a narcissistic investment in his own body, the castration threat, against his incestuous desire in the familial complex, he will always choose to salvage his narcissism and turn away from his desire. But this is no solution. It still leaves the question of desire hanging in the balance. It seems that the child must come to terms with incestuous desire and abandon a narcissism that can only be a way station on the path toward desire for other objects.

For Lacan, a work of mourning must take place. In the case of the boy, for example, to desire his mother leaves him vulnerable to the threat of his father's punishment, while on the other hand, to be the object of his father's desire leaves him likewise castrated since he is in the feminine position. However you render this story, sexuality, having a body, conflicting gender identifications, locating yourself in the generational turn, have a significant impact that requires signification.

The temptation to resolve these through being the object of desire (rather than the complicated subject of it) is a problem that Lacan called the problem of being the phallus for the Other—wanting to be for them what they are irrevocably lacking. Mourning means confronting this lack.

The phallus is a fantasy whose origin is signification itself—what comes in the place of absence. Fantasy tries to fix signification or reduce it to a static image—one signifier, the signifier one. All object relations are inherently fetishistic, as Freud says in *The Three Essays* (1905a). This is how Lacan reads the importance of the *bedrock of castration*—the encounter with impossibility and limit, with the failure of the phallus, that initiates the dissolution of the Oedipus Complex. "Castration, I say it is real!" said Lacan.

With Lacan, desire, its interminable movement, is itself the limiting factor in so far as it draws you toward the castration complex. Psychoanalysis at its best pushes the patient as far as is possible across the threshold of his narcissism, the limits of his own identity, traversing the fantasy in the direction of desire. Lacan traces this to Freud in *The Interpretation of Dreams (1900)*, when he says that one can locate an end to interpretation particularly when the desire to master the dream, to know it in full, in effect, dies out. Does the dream create this limit or is the limit one that allows us to truly get inside the dream? The answer, if there is one, probably extends beyond the simplicity of this either or. For Freud, in any case, this endpoint of interpretation was referred to as the *omphalos*. It evokes both origin and cut.

Lacan said that in analysis one person believes that something is impossible and it can never be the analyst. If the analyst refuses something, it is most likely the anxiety that the analysand demands of him as a way of avoiding castration. Like the demand for consistency, the analysand is brought in the direction of that which threatens it. This is always a logical move. "Logic is defined in the field where the subject supposed to know is brought to nothing" (Lacan, 1971a, Lecture X, p. 15). Unconscious fantasy manifestly is always a stated impossibility that harbors its opposite—the narcissistic *pathos*. The analyst's faith in the unconscious is situated as the direct inversion of this principle.

Psychoanalysis is the unique act of finding our way with our unconscious, finding our way with desire, putting the unconscious to work as our instrument. We have little else that is truly ours. It is this know-how with desire that Lacan felt appeared in the analysis as a formal writing that was inherently transformative. He elevates this as the aim.

When I first went into analysis I only had one kind of dream—no memories, one dream. They were, on the whole, underwater dreams. I would be swimming and looking. I only understood this much later, but the act of looking was directly tied to the swimming. The feeling of being submerged and suspended is what allowed me to look with a sense of calm. Looking, no less being looked at, was not something that in my day to day life engendered ease. So follows the wish in the dream.

In fact looking might have been my greatest source of anxiety manifesting itself once in a strange symptom at the very beginning of analysis where I had to leave for a period of time because I didn't like the way my analyst looked at me. At the same time I had a paradoxical feeling that he couldn't look at me, and one might surmise in this a desire to be looked at. This is all well and fine, analysis brings to the surface these vicissitudes, and they are, in the case of a good enough analysis, weathered, if not elaborated.

The incestuous tie is certainly there in these quasi-*uterine* dreams and the transitory phobic symptom. Lacan's brilliant insistence on reading the Oedipal in the preoedipal is instructive. It is not just the boundless narcissism of the watery expanse, the archaic mother of the Thalassa complex, or the death drive as a uterine calm, nor even the narcissistic voyeuristic complex, it is these too, but what these mask or block that is of utmost importance. The phobia certainly betrays that more is at stake, no less the pole of excitement that is always curiously missing in any sense of calm.

Being in analysis disturbed, to say the least, this particular sense of calm—at least for a while. The underwater dreams vanished for a period of years and I had nothing but nightmares. Buried in these nightmares were always the most tender of wishes and it took a great deal of work, perhaps mostly on the side of my analyst, to get me past a sense of horror or disgust in order to say or see something more. Such is the terror of recognizing one's own desire.

It is the dream of *the memorial* and the dream of *the vase and the letter* that together emerged as a different mode of representation after a time of analytic work. From an absolute, almost dead calm, from the position of the passive voyeur, to the more actively experienced nightmares and a horrified fascination with scenes of imminent violence, there is still something about desire that remains split-off or submerged. In fact, I might say that it was in representing to myself impossibility in the dream of the memorial (*no one can*), certainly on the edge of a scene of violence and a calm initiated by the tortured memorial, that elaboration was first opened outward. Perhaps the memorial stood in for this way of representing my subjective place—outside safe, inside lost.

So it is not that these former ways of representation are not mine, of course they are mine, but I do not quite have a place within their structure. It is not as if I am not looking, or fascinated, or horrified, in these other dreams you have read, but there these are moments in a whole field of meanings, memories, representations, and wishes that serve as a series of co-ordinates. It is perhaps important to know that it is only after this shift that I was in fact able to remember anything at all of my early life, notably perhaps the time I spent as a young girl, just before the dissolution of my family, playing in the water with my father.

If I were to try and say what I think Lacan gives to his female audience, it is his elevation of the feminine, the *not-all*, Other *jouissance*, as the only place which can break new ground. Love and knowledge must aim for this beyond as the ground on which to break. In his way, Lacan gives what he does not have. The nothing that is "the destiny and drama of love" (Lacan, 1986/1992, p. 256). This radical opening is linked to both an effect of the word, woman, and the possibility of sublimation as afforded by analysis:

> But it is indeed something different that is in question. It is the opening, it is the gap onto this radically new thing that every cut of the word introduces. Here it is not only from the woman that we have to wish for this grain of phantasy or this grain of poetry, but from analysis itself (Lacan, 1958, L1.7.59, p. 435)

Certainly it was after the years of nightmares that something broke open and we might wonder what this has to do with femininity, no less Oedipus.

I can't say that at the time I was happy to be relieved of my dreams of swimming and what sustained me was only the slightest faith that the analysis would come to something else with which I would be better off. I laugh thinking about it now. This problem surfaced, I think unbeknownst to either of us, in the transference. I tortured my analyst, no less myself, for months, insisting that I wanted to be a scuba-diver and not a psychoanalyst. Could he just say that that was ok? I would be cured, I insisted. I would be happy. You cannot go back the silence seemed to insist.

The all-loving, omnipresent father must fall. It is only here, in the fall to where he is not-all, that we can encounter the abyss. Like the fascinated child, the mute princess, and the criminal mother, what you win by way of knowledge you instantly lose. She will retain her desire as a question. Lacan, despite his pleas, knew this. And he knew the women would never give anything like *answers;* that what they know is perhaps only about what cannot be known. In asking women to speak, he reverses his position and makes the audience his analyst. Say what you know! Tell me the secrets of desire!

Some of the work that I would encounter in analysis many years later, during a more quiescent period of my life, was what it was that I was seeking in the water. The time I spent on beaches, in the ocean, aroused an intense desire to look and find, turning over rocks, seeking in nooks and crannies. I had to withstand a kind of terror in this exploration. How could you put your hand in there? All of the imagined culprits would multiply. I tested my courage. But it was never what was found—rocks, shells, small animals—that seemed to matter, but to find a way to continue looking, despite fear, disappointment, or even success.

I often couldn't bear for this game to end, and indeed, it doesn't have to, in which case not ending it also becomes a problem. I played with how to stop—when the bucket is full, three more of these, when I've found something I haven't seen before. Which one could be a desired end? Which one allowed for another beginning? How quickly? When does beginning again lag behind desire, or when does desire lag behind already having found oneself in the act? Psychoanalyst's who work with children know how this structuring of games seems to encompass so much of what we do in play. It is a way of mapping how desire lives and dies.

The little traumas of life give us an opportunity to rework this entire fabric of being—who we have been and who we will come to be after a given event. Often enough there are problematic snags in this process of stretching one's identity—between what is no longer and what is not yet, like the reaching suspension in the process of signification. It can fill one with a sense of horror. Perhaps analysis allows us to encounter this movement, its ebbs and flows, with a little more ease. Perhaps in analysis, what we do is live through this impossible restructuring of our unconscious desire, always connected to the intensification of the transference.

My father, after my mother left, and subsequently after their divorce, never took me on holiday again. Would I have dreamt of water so readily if this hadn't been the path of these experiences? Perhaps not, but as memories one might imagine that they have enough resonance on their own. Was it necessary for these dreams to be so extreme with respect to their cloak and dagger operation with desire? Necessary? Certainly one might hope not, but what is necessary? Whatever takes the unnecessary, which encompasses the majority of life, and makes of it a kind of necessity, a need to find one's way, however painful, I imagine we should take on board.

A symptom is certainly something that takes an early scene, the efflorescence of desire in Oedipal childhood say, and colors it with the traumas of life. The pleasure is only a danger thereafter, relegated to a world of dreams where it is effectively lived in disguise. It would take what felt like an eternity of nightmares to recover what was left of my desire, split-off in this way. It is strange to know that it is a very simple absence or loss that sets off this chain of events when all is said and done. Yet, when all is said and done, getting closer to the effects of a *simple absence* on the entire composition of a life is something I wouldn't easily barter away, even if that could have been the price of my nightmares. Perhaps this simple absence is one way of thinking through this question of the feminine. The dreams in this book, like the formation of a signature, are perhaps always, when all is said and done, feminine.

There is one story in the aftermath of these that I would like to tell. Once, when contemplating the idea of what it would be like to be back in analysis, I thought about how horrible I felt during much of it and this particular early moment of an infinity of nightmares. To hell with going through that again, I balked, not on your life. And pay for it? Money is always a good means of final resistance—we won't sacrifice it for the world.

With some temperance by virtue of time, I thought about whether it would have to be like that a second time? Is there any way to know in advance? Trying to know like this seems wrong. Shouldn't I know better? Maybe I do need more analysis. I went to sleep with these questions lingering in my mind, also mildly annoyed that I could feel so repugnant toward something that remains critical to what I do, who I am.

That night I had the first nightmare in what must have been five years or so. I was on my spiral staircase in my house and I reached back into my hair with my hands and encountered the remains of a dead spider. A chill ran through my body—I was increasingly petrified. I didn't want to touch it, but how could I not, at the very least, to excise its presence. I managed, somehow, god knows, in this state of mortification to find a thought. I remember saying to myself—what could be worse than finding a dead spider in your hair, at which point, just as the thought concluded, an alive one crept around the other side of my face and reared its legs. I woke up with a gasp of breath.

Within a few seconds I ended up bursting into laughter. The dream was a perfectly structured joke: What could be worse than finding a dead spider in your hair? Finding an alive one! So the nightmare was a reminder of what I found in analysis—desire, a question of life and death, the reversal between tragedy and comedy, a sense of humor, the formal beauty of a wish. What are you afraid of, what can I know, also perhaps my annoyance with myself, found their answer.

Spiders have always symbolically been linked to the feminine, and while I might not have bothered with associations—wasn't the laugh enough—and in particular with such grossly generalized ones as this, there is something of importance here to note. The site on the stairs is a place where my mother had recently fallen down and certainly the conflict between mothers and daughters, this mother and myself, is bound up with this scene, no less the original scene of analysis. Is she worse dead or alive? If I may put it in that interrogative form. And further, one cannot really make a choice like this when it comes to life and death, no less mothers. More than this, I would say that the dream, responding to thoughts about not wanting to live through certain moments again in analysis, says something about its bedrock—this encounter with one's horror of femininity. It was a reminder that I *am* in fact grateful that I continue to be both horrified and good humored.

A horror of femininity

"Is she worse dead or alive?" is a question that is asked in its own way by Hamlet about himself—to be or not to be. Hamlet's words circle around the question of life and death, action and inaction, the integrity of the object or its debasement and dissolution. "That this too solid flesh would melt, thaw, and resolve itself into a dew" … as he says in his first soliloquy. The question of death and mourning, Lacan points out, runs from one side of the play to the other. No one in this play speaks about anything but death and mourning. The encounter with the ghost is nothing other than the encounter with death itself, which causes a profound estrangement in Hamlet.

Gertrude mourns her husband, Hamlet's father, too quickly; Hamlet is accused by his father's murderer, his uncle Claudius, of mourning too long; Ophelia, whose father is buried in stealth after being murdered by Hamlet, descends into a melancholic madness; and, Laertes, like Hamlet, loses both his father and Ophelia, both men competing over their grief in a struggle that curiously takes place in Ophelia's very grave. The play, Lacan says, ends in a pile of corpses. It is not our own death—which is something no one has—but the death of others that tears the very fabric of our being.

Just as Freud smuggles the Oedipus Complex into *The Interpretation of Dreams (1900)* in a section on dreams of the deaths of persons of whom one is fond—where Oedipus is positioned as the direct inversion of the story of Hamlet who bears out its inhibiting consequences in his character—there is something important to be wrestled with in this tragic play. Lacan's reading of Hamlet is a singular act of interpretation, disentangling the structure, form, and content of the play, loosening the bonds of hundreds of years of prior, often quite contradictory, interpretation.

Positioned between his 1957–1958 Seminar V, *The Formations of the Unconscious*, and the well-known 1959–1960 Seminar VII, *The Ethics of Psychoanalysis*, Lacan takes up the question of Hamlet in 1958–1959 under the heading, *Desire and Its Interpretation*. I think it is important to see this reading of Hamlet as following a question about the unconscious, and, as a prelude to his remarks on sublimation and the ethical integrity of desire in his reading of Antigone.

Hamlet is Antigone's tragic counterpart. Where he ends, she begins—notably as one who is marked and destined for death. Their difference hinges on their relation to their own will and desire. At the extreme end, Antigone, for Lacan, is an emblem of femininity, whereas Hamlet is described as being possessed by nothing short of an absolute horror of it. These two, taken together, tell us something about the action and aim of psychoanalysis unrivaled since Freud's own coupled reading of

Sophocles and Shakespeare. It is Lacan's insistence on a return to Freud that gave him the impetus to take up this original question that marks the terrain of the birth of the Oedipus complex.

The reading of Hamlet stretches over two months of seminars. Each session is like a successive pass over the entire play, repeated and repeating elaborations of a building structure that keeps looping back around in order to gain fresh momentum. When I read Lacan's seminars I almost have to find a state of consciousness that allows me to ignore the jargon, the bad translations, funneling my attention back and forth between the French and English, his text and the one he is commenting on, the difference between himself and Freud. I have to, as I have said, find a way to enjoy him and the unfolding of his words in a stretch of time that is not mine. It is not unlike the suspended attention that is demanded of the psychoanalyst.

In the case of Hamlet one might wonder if reading a play, I suppose like reading one of Lacan's transcripts—something that is supposed to be seen, witnessed, experienced, and heard, in a setting that takes place among others in a heightened state of attention—is impossible. Reading what is meant to be a spoken discourse requires an added feat of imagination. When I first began reading this seminar, I did so without any particular interest. At a second pass, I stopped short at an exclamation of Lacan's in his second session. It was a moment where I suddenly remembered that Lacan was speaking and I saw him there, saying what I was reading, in particular, saying it to an audience. It was a moment that I took to be unscripted, a surprise, even to him, perhaps only because of a reversal in an identification, a transitivity, where *I* was surprised.

This point of identification aside, it was *the* moment when I suddenly realized that we were in the midst of reading Hamlet and I wanted to know where Lacan was going to go with it:

> For those who read the text, it is something that knocks you over backwards, makes you bite the carpet and roll on the ground, it is something unimaginable. There is not a verse of Hamlet, nor one of his replies, which does not have in English a percussive power, a violence of language which makes of it something which one is at every moment absolutely stupefied. You could believe that it was written yesterday, that one could not write things like that three centuries ago (Lacan, 1958, L11.3.59, p. 8).

What knocks Lacan over backward? What has him biting the carpet and rolling around on the ground? What in Hamlet is so violent and unimaginable? What can we identify with so strongly even though it is centuries old? I'd be hard pressed not to recognize this as a moment of Lacan's desire that I encountered in such a way that it evoked my own.

I would say that this moment sets the tone for the entire reading of Hamlet. Whatever this percussive power, this stupefaction, Lacan goes on to say, the play unfurls like this—as if everyone has their back to a wall of truth that they cannot recognize and is hemming in on them from all sides. It is as if we are caught at a certain threshold where there is no relaxation. The world becomes a living reproach that they, and Hamlet best, are ensnared by. Hamlet's words seem to try to shatter this intolerable limit—words that become a cruelty he unleashes in all directions, perhaps always first at himself.

Nothing can be gained, nothing can wanted, this is the melancholic's nihilistic position. A cowardice in the face of life, an endless meditation on the object of action, as Hamlet says. For Lacan then, the violence of Hamlet, is the violence of failed mourning. Lacan conjectures that an intrinsic relation between time and mourning is staged in the very form of the play. Nothing is more out of joint in this play so much as time. Hamlet lives at an hour that is never his own, the time of his parents and of others to which he lends himself. Hamlet, chained to these others, endlessly procrastinates, only, in a burst of haste, to act with utter impulsivity. He is always too early or too late. Thought and action, words and deeds, are interminably at odds. The play seems to veer around disjointed moments: its long drawn out beginning only for Hamlet to be gone for months, with a final mad sequence of events where all parties meet their end.

If there is a difference between Oedipus and Hamlet the difference is one between action and inhibition. You only act when you do not know—that you've killed your father and are sleeping with your mother—and when you do know, the consequence of that knowledge is a morbid inhibition. "The one who knows is in such a dangerous position as such, so marked out for failure and sacrifice, that he has to take the path, as Pascal says somewhere, of being mad along with the others" (Lacan, 1958, L15.4.59, p. 12), in other words, pretending again not to know. The truth that Hamlet is exposed to—his mother is married to his father's murderer, his father's brother—is a hopeless truth, a truth without much redemption. If it doesn't make one mad to begin with, like Ophelia, then one has to play a game of madness.

How can we identify with someone as problematic as Hamlet, Lacan asks? Why is the pinnacle of an actor's career so often to play him? T. S. Eliot (1920/1997) famously called the play an aesthetic failure and yet it marks a critical turn in Shakespeare's work from the pastoral comedies to plays that, Lacan says, are a quantum leap from these. What is it in this play that can act as such a turning point? Hamlet, to put it quite simply, evokes what Lacan calls the tragedy of desire "in so far as man is not simply possessed, invested by it, but that he has to … find this desire. Has to find it at all costs, and in great suffering, to the point of not being able to find it except at the limit" (Lacan, 1958, L11.3.59, p. 9).

This limit for Lacan is the limit of the self, of one's narcissism, which must be traversed. Mourning is the pivot between narcissism and desire. This narcissistic capture that Hamlet embodies—this locked, internal tension of inhibition and the sense of injury—shows us the necessity of desire; it's point of relief. However, what this desire represents is a tragic and painful passage through the process of mourning. Death is always the horizon of this self-shattering, loss is always in the background of any work with desire.

Hamlet shows us that loss is felt with such tortuous shame and humiliation that we retreat into ourselves. It is often only first through others that we take in the image of ourselves, that we begin to recover desire at all—a little like this moment of hearing Lacan's desire to read the play in which I suddenly experience my own. We need these mirror-others as a support, and too much Otherness will unleash a fury of anxiety and aggression. It is this drama of desire—between the safety of like others and a terrifying unknown—that Lacan begins to outline through this play, exemplary of the dialectical unfolding of desire through narcissism as he metaphorized it in the mirror-stage.

Hamlet must be given back his desire—its ardor, its grief, its singular history. Through others, he tests desire, from his mother, to his step-father, Ophelia, and Laertes—this last acting like Hamlet's double. These figures stand like our two sets of objects in psychic life: the primary objects that are one's parents, and the secondary ones of lovers and rivals. The play alternates between these; they structure Hamlet's tragic oscillation.

The play's conclusion is initiated when Hamlet, watching Laertes mourn at Ophelia's funeral, leaps at him in her grave, letting out an other-worldly cry of grief, declaring, "It is I, Hamlet the Dane." Through his double—Laertes embodying his narcissistic image—he is able to find something of his desire in a moment of seeing himself, outside of himself, positioned in relation to this lost object. Hamlet says:

> That to Laertes I forgot myself,
> For by the image of my cause I see
> The portraiture of his. I'll court his favors.
> But sure the bravery of his grief did put me
> Into a tow'ring passion.

Like the play within the play, we access something as intimate as desire in a moment outside of ourselves—in a flash identification. His grief, Lacan says, is found here for the first time. In saying I, Hamlet finally assumes his place as his father's son.

This is the very structure of theater—the audiences' relationship to this play itself and with Hamlet in particular. In part, it explains the importance of this encounter with Lacan's desire when reading the seminar on Hamlet. Falling down backward, biting things and rolling around, because of a certain violence at the heart of desire, of suffering, of the beauty of language, is found through him when he enunciates it with a kind of inimitable passion. In minimal form, it is something like a beginning triangulation, Hamlet-Lacan-myself, Hamlet-Laertes-Ophelia. Through rivalry over an object of desire, we gain some movement and traction.

So for Lacan, the basic thesis of Freud's that Hamlet cannot punish his uncle for what he has wished for unconsciously, is, as I hope you can see, more complicated than this. We should, Lacan suggests, take up this path that Freud points to and ask what is this unconscious of Hamlet and what is it that touches our own unconscious in the unfolding of the play. Hamlet idealizes his father, who has dispatched him to pursue justice in his name, and Hamlet is also perversely possessive of his mother, who has bedded down with this criminal uncle whom Hamlet calls a king of shreds and patches. Lacan asks, why would these two ones make zero?

Hamlet's absolute horror of femininity—linked to a failure to mourn and the turn toward narcissism—is crucial to unfolding what is amiss.

Ophelia, Lacan says, is the embodiment of this femininity, and as such, she is the play's casualty. If Hamlet's identification with Laertes served as an opening onto desire, Ophelia is in the reverse position. Her desire acts like an obstacle. In fact, not only Hamlet, but also most others in the play—Polonius, Laertes, and the king and queen also—dismiss that Ophelia is a subject with her own desire. She is taken as a pure object, as "bait". No one ever asks her what it is that she wants. They never encounter her in the dimension of her own desiring. In her madness we see this desire explode onto the scene, her subjectivity immersed in a sexuality impugned from the beginning. From this, she slips into the river and dies. The scene is described through her dress, mermaid like and without distress it became heavy with drink. In this play, we are never very far from the dimension of orality, which I am beginning to suspect is why it has Lacan biting the carpet. Nowhere is the play more orally violent than in the encounter between Hamlet and his women.

Ophelia acts as a barometer throughout the play for Hamlet's position with respect to his desire, says Lacan. Through her we find out about his wild estrangement, gone half-mad, after the encounter with his father's ghost. After that encounter, Hamlet can do nothing but violently reject Ophelia—he has no desire for her any longer. It is only in her death, in the scene with Laertes just described, that Hamlet is in any possession of it again. The play seems to turn around her.

Lacan says that Ophelia has become for Hamlet, in his despair, "the pure and simple support of a life which in its essence becomes condemned for Hamlet. In short, what is produced at that moment, is this destruction or loss of the object which is reintegrated into the ego in its narcissistic framework" (Lacan, 1958, L15.4.59, p. 15). Hamlet's melancholia causes a regression toward narcissism. Narcissism literally pulls desire inward, into the ego, as Freud outlines in *Mourning and Melancholia* (1917). The destruction of the world in melancholic sadness, its profit and texture, is the cost of this withdrawal of desire, which is the only thing that sustains our relation to the world. Without it, the world is flat, and Ophelia collapses into this object that Hamlet repudiates in the form of her femininity—"get thee to a nunnery," "wouldst thou be a breeder of sinners," "I say we will have no mo marriage."

She is dissolved with such cruelty. The vicissitudes of her womanliness are attacked one by one. "She is herself a bud which is ready to blossom, and which is menaced by the insect gnawing at the heart of this bud. This vision of life ready to blossom, and of life which carries all lives, it is thus moreover that Hamlet qualifies it, situates it, in order to reject it" (Lacan, 1958, L 4.8.59, p. 12). Ophelia is this fecundity that is an offense, a breeder of sinners and calumny, a liar, a whore, and on the other side, always to be a chaste little girl. She is, Lacan says, what all girls are to men in the blossom of their youth—a phallus.

What is this object that Ophelia is that promotes this unfolding action in Hamlet? "Ophelia is one of the most fascinating creations which has been proposed to human imagination. Something which we can call the drama of the feminine object, the drama of desire, of the world which makes its appearance at the dawn of civilization in the form of Helen … incarnated in the drama and misfortune of Ophelia" (Lacan, 1958, L 4.3.59, p. 10). When Ophelia dies, she is given the sign of impossibility. She is literally evoked as lost—the lost, errant object that is at the dawn of civilization. Hamlet, through her death, confronts a desire that must be bound by loss, and finally begins to grieve. Her death acts like a second encounter with death that allows something of his own mourning to finally begin taking place.

But there is one more woman we must speak about and she is quite a woman at that. Ophelia is coupled with Gertrude, and their interplay is the play of a displacement of rage from mother to would-be-wife. Lacan famously said (with some impetuousness that many found offensive) that Gertrude is a gaping cunt. Mourning means nothing to her—when one goes, another comes. The question of the mother's desire is a question about mourning, of a mourning transmitted between generations that must be assumed or accomplished. There must be something found beyond the image, especially beyond this image of a mother whose desire is only for her own satisfaction.

This is the same beyond that we see Hamlet try and fail to elevate in relation to Ophelia. Hamlet is looking for desire beyond *jouissance*—desire in the name of king and country, in the name of virtue and beauty, we might say, in the name-of-the-father. This attempt always reaches a sheer pitch of idealization from which it sinks back down—into filth, into rags, into shreds and patches. This splitting of the object, Lacan says, has its concomitant in the fading of the desire of the subject.

He wants to elevate their desire toward something beyond themselves. Without this beyond, an oral, greedy wanton desirousness which he sees in them seems to threaten him. With transitivity worthy of Lacan's mirror stage, every reproach against his mother will reverse into a self-reproach: "Bloody, bawdy villain! Remorseless, treacherous, lecherous kindless villain … Why, what an ass am I! This is most brave, that I … must like a whore unpack my heart with words, and fall a cursing like a very drab, a scullion!" The cause, the problem, is not, Lacan says, Hamlet's unconscious desire for his mother, it is his mother's desire that poses a problem for Hamlet.

With the death of his father Hamlet is thrown back upon the desire of his mother in a melancholic identification with her. He cannot separate. Lacan is reinterpreting Freud's statement that in melancholia the shadow of the object has fallen on the ego. Hamlet is crushed by his mother's desire at every step—"Must I remember? Why, she would hang on him as if increase of appetite had grown by what it fed on … frailty thy name is woman," he says with bitter irony.

When Hamlet speaks, what he says always seems to slip from his place into his mothers. He speaks only to imagine his mother with Claudius, to remember her love for his father, to ruminate on her injuriousness to him, to ponder her desire in its tempo and flush. If his mother pleads with him in the opening scene, "let not thy mother lose her prayers, Hamlet," then his answer, "I shall in all my best obey you, madam," is the one oath that Hamlet sustains. "Nothing in him can oppose in short a sort of fundamental availability … hiring himself to another and again for nothing" (Lacan, 1958, L 4.22.59, p. 6).

Ultimately, he never confronts his mother with the truth that he has learned from the ghost of his father. She learns it only as she dies. It is only after Hamlet sees Gertrude die that he learns of his own poisoning, and only in the short interval between this wound and his own death, will he finally avenge his father's murder. He proceeds, to the very end of the play, in lockstep with his mother's desire. Desire, for Lacan, must cut through this mirroring melancholic identification. Some act of mourning must cut through this pride of injury in relation to his mother.

The ghost, Lacan says, is this cut. The ghost of Hamlet's father always appears to intervene in the space of this cut, between Hamlet and his mother—beseeching Hamlet not to, to step back, to purify his desire of this preoccupation, to remember his duty there where he needs to most, namely in the face of his mother. The ghost pleads with Hamlet to hear him—"lend thy serious hearing"; "so art thou to revenge, when thou shalt hear"; "now, Hamlet, hear"—and then leaves him with one imperative: "howsoever thou pursuest this act; taint not thy mind nor

let thy soul contrive against thy mother aught: leave her to heaven."
Hamlet, to be sure, cannot hear this message of the ghost.

It appears again and for the last time in the incestuous scene with
his mother. The reading of this scene is the heart of Lacan's interpretation of Hamlet. After staging the play within the play—something
that should alert us of an important turning point—Hamlet catches
Claudius defenseless in a moment of prayer and *does not kill him.*
He has his evidence, his chance, and he procrastinates. It is "hire and
salary," he says, not revenge. Hamlet dreams of a moment of purify-
ing violence, interrupting Claudius in a moment of incestuous passion,
cutting him off in the blossom of his sin like his father was—a primal
scene fantasy if there ever was one. Whatever it is about this fantasy,
it gives him the impetus not to act, and instead, he goes to his mother.
If there is something inexplicable about this stepping down, the inhibition that washes over Hamlet, we will learn of it in this scene with his
mother.

"And there takes place this long scene which is a kind of highpoint
of the theater, this something about which the last time I told you that
to read it brings you to the limit of what you can tolerate, where he is
going to adjure his mother pathetically to become aware of the point
that she is at" (Lacan, 1958, L 3.18.59, p. 12). Once he reaches her in her
chambers, Hamlet, in an act of rash haste, kills Polonius asking if it is
the king—whom we know he has just left outside. It is as if this fantasy
has gotten the best of him.

He then begins his appeal to Gertrude, that she should know and
temper her desire—a message also no doubt meant for himself given
in this inverted form. "O shame, where is thy blush? Rebellious hell, if
thou canst mutine in a matron's bones, to flaming youth let virtue be as
wax and melt in her own fire. Proclaim no shame." His words mount
in tension and violence and Gertrude literally writhes beneath them.
As she cries for Hamlet to say no more, that he has cleft her heart in
twain, the ghost suddenly appears:

> Do not forget. This visitation
> Is but to whet thy almost blunted purpose.
> But, look, amazement on thy mother sits.
> O, step between her and her fighting soul!
> Conceit in weakest bodies strongest works.
> Speak to her, Hamlet.

If Gertrude has no shame, this conceit cannot be matched by Hamlet's own with which he mirrors her—her desirous excess and his aggressive one. Step between her and her fighting soul, the ghost asks, stepping into this space between her and him. Speak to her, the ghost implores.

"This place where Hamlet is always being asked to enter, to operate, to intervene, is here something which gives us the real situation of the drama. And despite the intervention, the signifying summons. It is signifying to us [psychoanalysts] because this is what is in question for us, what intervening means for us: 'Between her and her', that is our work. 'Conceit in weakest bodies strongest works', it is to the analyst that this appeal is addressed" (Lacan, 1958, L3.11.59, p. 15). The ghost, if I may put it like this, is the one who ushers a cut like the psychoanalyst. It asks Hamlet to step into a space, into the cut of this in-between, into the interval of desire. Between you and you, this is what the psychoanalyst offers. Conceit in weakest bodies strongest works, this is what our patients tell us.

Hamlet will only find this space in the form of a literal wound, a mortal cut. He cannot hear the message of the ghost any more than he can speak to his mother. What follows this scene with the ghost, Lacan says, is one more act of stepping down where we see the disappearance, the dying away of his appeal—"laying down his arms before something which seems ineluctable to him; namely that the mother's desire here takes on again for him the value of something which in no case, and by no method, can be raised up" (Lacan, 1958, L 3.18.59, p. 13). And he sends her back to Claudius, tells her to let him kiss her neck, call her his little mouse, and denounce Hamlet as mad. He literally collapses into her, speaking not from the position of "I, Hamlet," but from her position, what she will be for Claudius and Claudius for her.

At this intersection between body and identification, ideals and their problematic immateriality, Hamlet must locate his desire. Lacan turns our attention to what Hamlet says in his feigned madness after killing Polonius and stashing the body beneath the stairs: the body is with the king, but the king is not with the body; the king is a thing, a thing of nothing. "I would ask you to replace the word King by the word phallus in order to see that it is precisely what is in question, namely that the body is engaged in this affair with the phallus, and how, but on the contrary, the phallus itself is not engaged in anything … it always slips between your fingers (Lacan, 1958, L 4.29.59, p. 15). The phallus,

Lacan declares, is a ghost—nothing but a shade. Crossing the castration complex means bearing this news, enduring its cut.

The dissolution of the Oedipus complex is this crossing between narcissism and desire, melancholia and mourning, tied to a question of the phallus. There is no happy success in this, and perhaps the tragedy of Hamlet is the staging of this difficulty. The Oedipus complex, as Freud tirelessly shows, leaves behind its wounds, its scars, in the form of the castration complex. When we come to the end of this affair, the exigencies of love—the "mother" being the first object of this demand, the "father" the first ideal—the loss in this is always radical. From this perspective, Lacan says, we can see the most radical position of the subject in the very negativity of this loss. Either this phallus disappears through the act of mourning, or it is desire.

One virtue is enough

The ethical figure for Lacan is embodied by Antigone. She puts herself beyond fear, beyond pity, beyond nostalgia even, and the boundary point for her is always that between life and death. Her object is "the still living corpse" that she seeks to animate with her desire. Antigone, he says, "even refers to the image of Niobe, who is imprisoned in the narrow cavity of a rock and will be forever exposed to the assault of rain and weather." It is "around this image of the limit that the whole play turns" (Lacan, 1986/1992, p. 268). Antigone, in pushing toward this limit—maintaining her tie to a brother whose loss cannot be replaced, must be acknowledged—embodies the potential virtues of the analyst.

The ethical stance of the analyst initiates the unfolding cure, what Lacan calls the subversion of the feeding Other to the sexual Other, the autoerotic to the genital, the masochistic subject to the castrated one, from the discourse of the hysteric to that of the analyst. Nothing is to be refused in this discourse, not least of all, a patient's violent declaration of love. Psychoanalysis represents, at the extreme end of an ideal, a freedom of discourse—say anything, you must say everything.

For Lacan, fidelity to unconscious desire entails a certain kind of sacrifice or acceptance of castration—a giving up of the phallus. It does so in a particular setting, a setting that inherently carries varying characteristics of a kind of sacrifice—of all normative rules of discourse, of a wished for human relation, of cherished illusions, of money. Neurosis and perversion are particular structured ways of failing with respect to desire. In the latter, suffering and enjoyment condense in the figure of an essential hatred. Perverse hatred of this kind is without the possibility of the grace that Lacan hopes will come of desire. As he allegorizes it: "*I love you, but, because inexplicably I love in you something more than you … I mutilate you.*" Or, for the anal not oral variety, "*I give myself to you … but this gift of my person—as they say—Oh, Mystery! Is changed inexplicably into a gift of shit*" (Lacan, 1973/1981, p. 268).

As we have seen, knowledge, in relation to this freedom of discourse, always fails when it tries to tackle the question of sexuality. How had the sexuality of children escaped recognition for so long? And even to recognize it still leaves so many questions in its wake—Freud famously leaving behind his own in the form of the question, what does woman want? For Lacan, the castration complex is sexuality as this *felt* impossibility, as the encounter with impossibility. Perversion seeks to escape this—nothing is a problem, women have the phallus too.

Humanity, distributed between these poles, perversion-neurosis, one the negative of the other, is defined as the after-math of psychosexual development. Sexuality is to be reconciled by all, each in their own fashion, each by their very own symptom. We all bear the scars of this crossing. Lacan, like Adorno, with a faith in the work of a certain kind of negativity, will show no recourse to utopian ideals, sentimentality, or normative morality. Nostalgia is at root a way of avoiding the consequences of sexuality.

The task for Freud was to do something with what was given, particularly as an act of prolonging or continuing. The unconscious painfully raises the level of tension. Like Antigone, we must find a way to sustain the tension of desire. Fixations, inhibition, stasis, like empty repetition, are the real enemies. Nothing more. All life is a detour on the way to death. The specter of death raises its head at the moment when the unconscious fails to be put to work. Defense is always a defense against this unconscious act.

Love and marriage, Lacan says with some humor, are at the center of civilization and its neurotic discontents. My patients complain of nothing else. There is no knowledge that can suture the relation between the sexes and the discontent of marriage is the predicament, the tragedy even, of unconscious desire. Here is one place where Adorno's and Lacan's antiessentialism meet. We are not advocates for love and marriage, we hold to their impossibility. The hysteric arrives on the scene to represent a discontent with this discontent—love, marriage and family—at times a demand for something beyond its failure, and at other times, perhaps more analytic ones, a demand that one observe the law of this impasse as the condition for any overcoming.

Under this injunction, ethics coincides with epistemology. Epistemology is the counterpart question of any ethics of psychoanalysis. Their coincidence is perhaps in their absolute divergence, and this speaks to the important question of the limits of psychoanalysis. Today we are faced with the most spectacular contradictions concerning the epistemological basis of psychoanalysis. Does this threaten the unique ethical foundation of our work? At the very least, it displaces the question of ethics and having done so, risks replacing it with a question of mastery.

I have been asking about the transmission of psychoanalysis. What is the analytic process? How does one become a psychoanalyst? Lacan defined it as a kind of emptying out: the draining of the signifier (the past), a subversion of the pathos of suffering (present), and the fall of the overvalued or idealized object of love (the future). The precariousness of this process must be handled with tact. It is the declaration that one "cannot live in any other way," mirroring an original symptom (I cannot live, and no doubt, in any other way) which made the same declaration in the service of suffering. Be this, as Lacan says, or be nothing.

Thus he defines the ethic of the analyst: We will forge for ourselves "a quite different ethic, an ethic that would be founded on the refusal of being unduped, of always being more strongly the dupe of this knowledge, of this unconscious which, when all is said and done is our only lot in terms of knowledge" (Lacan, 1973, p. 16). We should always be more strongly the dupe of the unconscious. The debt that psychoanalysis engages in with respect to the unconscious must remain. It cannot be paid off.

Even in knowing this, one must, as a psychoanalyst, still find a way to take this risk. For the wager to retain its character as a wager, we have to find ourselves in the middle of it. We must continue, analyzed or not, to find a way to recoil with horror at the lever we use in our work as psychoanalysts. I cannot but somehow believe that what has been lost in psychoanalysis is this character of risk, and, the humility that it paradoxically carries with it. This can always be found in Lacan, signposted by the words failure, weakness, stupidity, the dummy, and the dupe. This he sees as the path of greater risk and greater gain.

Truth, Lacan says, has feminizing effects. He means this with a tinge of irony, but perhaps we still accept this idea of the virtue of a certain kind of courage in the face of weakness. It is not an easy task to keep one's eyes on the ephemeral. There is only one virtue for Lacan, *pudeur*, which one may translate as one likes—shame, decency, humility, modesty, prudence. Hopefully, without failing to hear the reference to the female genital.

As analysts, the cultivation of a lack of anxiety is indispensable. We are supposed to be able to withstand a certain amount of tension. American psychoanalysis labels this the maintenance of narcissistic equilibrium or the regulation of self-esteem. This is no doubt true, but such an idea would send the Lacanians into hysterics because this is precisely for them what the analyst must risk. Is this an issue of substance or terminology? Again it is always a question of how one constructs this limit and its beyond.

To return for a second to the new breed of Lacanians—I find their anxiety just as intolerable as that of the Americans, which might in fact be their double. The word of Lacan, brandished as the truth, makes true the very charge of intellectualism leveled against them from day one by the other side. The signifier is now something that is somehow both asserted with force and entirely discarded in favor of a theory of the *Real*. The real and the signifier function not as signifiers themselves—conceptual tools in an unfolding elaboration of the project of psychoanalysis—they function as a sign. What they mean to say, what they sign, is always the same: it is the name Lacan through which they demonstrate their allegiance to the master.

I might say that I follow Lacan because I don't really know what it is to be Freudian anymore, in particular, from the vantage point of a psychoanalyst in America. If Lacan only wanted to be called a Freudian, then I will say that I am Lacanian in the only way that someone who stands so far outside a discourse can claim that interior for herself— with total belligerence. A predicate come ethical subject.

If Lacan's ethics starts *ex nihilo*, is grounded through desire in a faith in almost nothing, emptying the future of content, audacity is a testimony to ethics. The words reserve, precariousness, grace, come from the attempt to conceptualize this place of impossible opening—a narrow crack in a rock. These virtues, rather than merely a consequence, an effect of analysis, are also its driving force.

"My strength," said Lacan, "is to know what it means to wait." Against the weighty seduction of the hysteric, against the defensive angst of the obsessive, the analyst must wait. It is the strength of a passive ideal that is never bound up with the immoderate nature of knowledge. Repression is a testament against this character of knowing. Freud, as Rieff (1959) pointed out rather strongly, never aimed at removing the bar of repression. Not because he thought man vile, but because repression is our saving grace. As with Freud's dream after his father's funeral (see, Freud 1900), I would say, you are requested to close an eye.

The analytic discourse is a discourse of tact, and, to quote Goethe, we have a better knowledge of things in knowing how *not* to try and know them so thoroughly. That the prudence of the analyst with respect to interpretation is all that the analyst has once he removes himself from the field of knowledge, challenges the notion of interpretation in its dimension of historical objectivity, "meaning making," transference dissolution, or any other such notion. It is all of these things, but more than these it is also a strategy:

> If analytic experience finds itself implicated by taking its claims to nobility from the Oedipal myth, it is indeed because it preserves the cutting edge of the oracle's enunciation, and I would say more, that in it interpretation always remains at the same level. It is only true by its consequences, like every oracle. Interpretation is not put to the test of a truth that can be settled by a yes or a no, it unleashes truth as such. It is only true insofar as it is truly followed (Lacan, 1971a, Lecture XII, p. 13)

This cutting edge of the oracle is the enunciation that gets things moving, which unleashes truth.

This is close to what Glover (1931) called the beauty of the inexact interpretation. As well, we have what are called the three T's of interpretation—tact, tone, and timing—in ego-psychology (Pine, 2001). For Lacan, since truth can only be half-said, all interpretations are inexact but beautiful, and all aim to be beautiful strategies of rhetoric. Beauty stands as the most important feature—hiding and revealing with exactly the right balance. How else would we allow ourselves to be led toward what is an unraveling, an undoing, a form of castration?

Knowing the difficulties of adding virtue to this series—castration, femininity, sacrifice, submission—let us remember that the word *pudeur* bears traces of the feminine. The nondupe, the nonpude, are not what we are as psychoanalysts. Let's call it, the indecent. Decency, for me, evokes the notion of shame in a powerful way, whereby, far from being a primitive affect, guilt seen as superior, it is directly related to the body. Here, we can understand something more about why it is always for Freud the affect of women *par excellence*. You can find it everywhere in his writing—their modesty, their shame, their secrecy, and powerful silences. The tie between this characterization and the position of the analyst is not an uninteresting one from my perspective.

Furthermore, Lacan takes this link and joins the question of the feminine to the question of writing. I believe that new forms of writing psychoanalysis most somehow rely on this ground and all else will be painfully secondary. Psychoanalysis must find a way to write again in a manner beyond professionalization, and this criticism is also directed at Lacan, who in fact wrote very little. The shift Lacan effects from the letter of Freud to his spoken voice, is vastly important—but it leaves in its wake the question of writing.

If there was this moment of *écriture feminine,* its moment has passed. What new reinvigoration of psychoanalysis at this level of the written is still possible? A question about sublimation hangs in the balance. "The Thing is not there originally. Sublimation brings us to it—this is the new" (Lacan, 1986/1992, p. 145). Sublimation is impossible without a certain kind of confrontation with impossibility. For now, that impossibility stands as the impossibility of psychoanalysis itself. Invest in its corpse. Reanimate this corpse as living. Love it in its utter uniqueness and impossibility.

Lacan joked with his audience in his 1972–1973 Encore Seminar, that all of what he had been saying about the "doesn't stop not being written" of the sexual relationship didn't mean that he didn't write plenty of notes in order to get up and speak about it. I would like to demand a supplement. If it is true that what we do in analysis is follow through without detour to the end of what we have to say, why would this not prepare us to write? What danger is there in relation to writing that is preventing new forms from developing?

Psychoanalytic writing cannot engender an effect of truth predicated on criteria of demonstrations and reiterations of knowledge and understanding. It excludes writing as such. In a dual movement—exclude nothing, exclude everything—psychoanalysis hedges its bets. To be excluded is the essence of woman. They complain of nothing else, Lacan (1975/1998) said in *Encore*. Exclusion always makes a wager more real—risking everything, one risks exclusion from everything.

Lacan, speaking about Antigone, says, "there is one thing that man hasn't managed to come to terms with and that is death, the Chorus says that he has come with an absolutely marvelous gimmick, namely, translated literally, 'an escape into impossible sickness' (Lacan, 1986/1992, p. 275). The gimmick is also our own. Perhaps we need to come to terms with the life and death of psychoanalysis. Perhaps what is terrifying about new forms of writing is that it holds, like so many of these stories, onto the very path of our own disappearance. The analyst falls from his place in the unfolding cure and why should it not be the case outside the consulting room?

I have learned through Lacan to always go by way of this radical debt. I take in more than I can possibly give back. My faith in semblance, in the unconscious, turns on a kind of risk—incur greater and greater debt as one always does in love, giving and taking with what one does not have. In effect, this is nothing new about me, but it is cast in a new light through Lacan. The problems I always faced were in wanting a way out, but Lacan teaches you that when you really find your way inside, there doesn't really seem to be a reason to leave anymore. What happens after that is inconsequential. Desire is a powerful antidote to fear. My failure will be where I finally succeed.

So I might, in the end, get out from under this disappointment with psychoanalysis after all. This debt may be the only insurance I have that I can escape from the trap of believing that either "they" or I have something solid to give. The ethics of psychoanalysis is an artful but immaterial business. Lacan's ethics, as it turns out, is an ethics that will always be internal to psychoanalysis, internal to its very theory. It requires nothing outside, and if this isn't a virtue, it at least gives one legs to stand on, with pleasure. So my debt is much less difficult to manage if not for the very reason that I enjoy its incursion. Lacan said, one's relationship to enjoyment is work.

I hope that through this reading of Lacan I have shown you something more about what this work entails. If it seems like a fantasy of sacrifice in the form of a sacrifice of fantasy—that would be a fair characterization. I don't really think that sublimation can be delinked from fantasy, nor from an elaboration of it, which inevitably means enduring or accepting some form of cut. Perhaps the humorousness in this fine line can be a point of leniency. It is at least the one that I have found that endures both with myself and with my patients. A cure is always on the cutting line between *pathos* and *ethos,* to say nothing of *bathos* as well.

This is more or less how I have learned to think through Lacan—to find room to breathe under the weight of his voice and his gaze. It is not a body of knowledge in the end, but knowledge of this body that fails, that laughs, that dreams, and risks everything. "When a slave redeems himself, he is master only in this—that he risks everything … It is here, in some way, that the function of the analyst offers something like the dawn" (Lacan, 1991/2007, p. 176).

CHAPTER THREE

Instructions on how to fell a tree

If whatever was so oppressive and tormenting in loving a thinker like Adorno was repeated for the love of Lacan, it seems to me that an adherence to a debt, rather than a denial of it, were the stakes of this affair. I think his work is different from Adorno's. For Lacan, this impossibility rendered affirmatively gives you your only bearings as a subject, no less a psychoanalyst. Through him one is permitted to attempt with passion an act that always involves in some way a renunciation (of narcissism, of knowledge), and he for one never assumes that such a sacrifice is easily made. For Lacan there is no erotic thrill or moralism attached to this act, always only offered as a possibility. If he focuses on it, it is because in his return to Freud these were the consequences, drawn out to their most extreme edge, of his discovery of unconscious desire.

Lacan tries to set up the conditions for what it might mean for any one of us to find a way beyond our own neurosis. He does this throughout his twenty-eight years of teaching, tracing the dilemma in a multitude of differing ways: from his re-reading of Freud, to his use of mathemes, philosophy, clinical forays, and his parables of art and literature. It is stunning to think of the ground one person was able to traverse, and even further, that he always did so in the company of others.

I have told you about the ways in which I had gotten lost in this immense terrain—the jargon, the split with the International, the militia of Lacanians at present. It felt like suffocating beneath the weight of an unknown presence, laden in the reading of seemingly endless transcripts. It was in learning to love him, always for Lacan, a gift of weakness, that I was able to take his thought in. To know him you have to let him pass through you, like the air that one breathes. It was one way that I was finally able to hear his ineluctable sense of humor. No other psychoanalyst can make you laugh like Lacan.

In the end, the question that I was left with was the question of writing. Certainly it is a question very much at the heart of the late Lacan. Beyond the arguments that already exist—those that trace the early Lacan of desire and speech to the late Lacan of *jouissance* and writing—I think it is important to understand the difficulty that a purely spoken discourse poses for its children. How do we, after Lacan, find a way to write psychoanalysis? From my own perspective, a certain sacrifice of Lacan felt necessary for me. In particular, to find what in him permitted his reader to do what he could not, to hear the promise that he left behind—the possibility of writing despite the unfortunate burden of knowing and of knowing him.

I have come to feel that Lacan's abandonment of writing gave too much strength to his voice. In contrast to this, the silence of the women in his audience begins to hold center stage. They become the psychoanalyst. The very act of writing, no less the difficulty after Freud, is a necessity for the psychoanalyst who has already spent good time finding their place in speech, toward making oneself heard in this way. Perhaps there was something important in returning psychoanalysis to its own frontier of spoken language. But having done so, Lacan increasingly seemed turned to the women in his seminar. He asked them to form an answer which, as we know, came from them in the form of an *écriture*.

Through writing, it seems to me that a problematic omniscience can be brought down to a whisper in the play of the written word and the elusive signature of an author on their work. At its best, writing imposes a certain loss on an author that is different from the one needed in order to speak in front of an audience. It is a different order of commitment.

I've wondered if it is in fact here that Lacan finally did not want to give in. That he asked his readers, to say nothing of his transcribers, to take too much care of his words—to mind them, to keep them always in mind. Perhaps he also asked them to mind, behave, and I would not be the first to pick up on this thread of dire mastery (Roustang, 1976/1982). If one looks at his writing, it seems to bear his stamp through this putative tone—a binding tie, an impossible demand for identification. Writing should act as a different kind of invitation. It is this invitation that is needed more than ever for any continued life of psychoanalysis.

So it is between these two dreams—my grandmother's letter, so close to her spoken voice, and dream about a book that I found and read—that I found something bearing this other invitation. The book felt like it was mine, unmistakably so, but its written quality disturbed the search for authorship. There is something quiet about this dream, silent almost, as if it tends toward that edge. And while the feeling of being myself is there, its softness seems to diminish the sharpness that usually comes of delimiting that space. There was a strange intimacy in the third person impersonal address. Here is the book: *Instructions On How to Fell A Tree. One has to use breath. Your eyes, hands and voice will be too disruptive to the rhythm necessary to bring it down.* That was it.

To begin, I woke fascinated with the image, though not in a way that solidified my gaze. The dream already seemed to undercut that possibility. The beauty of the object disrupted one's eyes as a looking force, as if a veil had been drawn. This veil, contrary to what we might imagine, did not seem to obscure the stakes of this call to fell.

Nevertheless, after a time I found myself chastising the dream—like a typical hysteric I'm mistaking a tree for the forest; she can hardly do with one, to say nothing of a whole series of them; what rest can you possibly find? It was in hearing myself in this way that the absurdity of the command in the dream book dawned on me.

This impossibility in proximity to an injunction—*one must use breath*—became a point of relief. Nothing seemed more natural than this: An image of grace, a way with desire, patience and tact. Psychoanalysis is the grace of a losing strategy. It is as if the injunction itself emptied out. Even with a sense of humor, the one that we said can surround most feelings of impossibility—felling with breath, the three little pigs and the big bad wolf.

In *The Interpretation of Dreams (1900)*, Freud tells us that plants are always close to a thought about genitals and intercourse. Given that the unconscious always seems to be close to such a thought as well, there seems to be a rather funny equivalence between the vegetal world and the unconscious. We might remember that Freud called the densest part of a dream the place where its wish sprouts up like a "mushroom from its mycelium" (p. 525). His book on dreams is perhaps always first a *botanical* one.

Perhaps we have fallen on something a little closer to the truth in setting off on this chain of thoughts that moves between nature and spirit, the weight of judgment and an immaterial point of relief, sexuality, and humor. There is something important about moving away from the immanence of judgment—the force of the super-ego. Even in the banal symbolism, plants equal genitals, we are taken a hair's breadth away from mere pathologizing.

This dream seems to open out in a way that leaves little room for judgment, and in fact it may be *this,* as a wish, that acts as the dreams motive force—a longing for the minimal difference between a beautiful image, a joke, and the invective force of the super-ego. This precarious space, so close to something as immaterial as rhythm and breath, is necessary to finally get things moving, to bring it down.

I cannot suddenly help but see the hysterical wish to castrate the master and how it just barely succeeds in not being just that. In not being that, one would have to begin to see her virtues, to hear the *juste* in the just of just barely. The other side of failure, Lacan said, is this just barely succeeding which is how an analysis finishes. The fall, evoked by this kind of artifice—this leap through what is only the semblance of an instruction, a dream object—delimits a new starting point, constitutes a break. The other movements—the hands, voice, and eyes—were rather the force of stasis held in place by the object that never-fails not to capture. That is to say, until it finally fails in just the right way.

This is what Lacan called the hysterical *à faire* (hearing affair), a to do with love, which holds out the possibility that she may find herself quite somewhere else after all is said and done. He says in his Seminar, *The Other Side of Psychoanalysis*, about Oedipus:

> What happens to him is not that the scales fall from his eyes, but that his eyes fall from him like scales … Is it not this very object that we see Oedipus being reduced, not to undergoing castration, but I would rather say, to being castration itself? Namely, what remains when one of the privileged supports of the object disappear from him in the form of his eyes (1991/2007, p. 156).

So rather than the tree being what falls in the end—certainly it was only a book of instructions which cannot guarantee its stated end—it is the support of a wished for act in the form of eyes, voice, and hands, that is given up. There was never the image of a fallen tree, just the act of reading, an intensification of rhythm, of breath, as everything fell around this tree and me.

Whatever one does, one does it on very little. Being castration, becoming castration itself, is close to the image of the psychoanalyst that Lacan maintained—the one who listens beyond the object presented to one's eyes, ears, or hands (the last encompassing the Freudian triad of objects handled, breast, feces, phallus).

In his work *The Function and Field of Speech and Language (1970/2006),* Lacan plays with the word *arbre,* or tree. It is always the classical example used to describe the separation between a signifier and the signified—writing tree for the former and drawing a tree for the latter.

What is important for him is not that one comes to substitute for the other, certainly language is founded on this basis, but to recognize the radical fact of this *barre,* or bar, that separates the two. It is a *barre* that stands between the word *arbre* and the thing itself. This is the lesson of psychoanalysis in the form of the consequences of Oedipus and castration. Only when we have given up trying to have full access to a thing from which we are barred, incest no doubt, can we learn to find a certain rhythm that is our own—precisely in an encounter with this limit. Language happens not because of a successful substitution but by virtue of a radical separation. This *barre-arbre* might allow us to write, perhaps to write something not unlike a book found in a dream.

BADIOU

The smile of my master

As Badiou says in "What Is Love?" (2000), thought depends on the impossibility of angels. I see Badiou, angel like, in all white—with his mysterious smile and self-avowed dignity. He knows the place that he holds in a long line of important French philosophers in whose path he has followed. Badiou is in the impossible position of the master. It cannot really be any other way. He bears the burden more or less well. The axiomatic nature of his work means, following Lacan, that it is only necessary that he authorize himself—and yet, he is authorized. He stands between the two impossible poles of desire and mastery.

His work is attracted to a realm just beyond that which desire inhabits and this attraction is both Badiou's virtue and his potential failing. Being the master, he cannot entirely dissociate himself from a mastery that is detrimental to this life of desire and whatever possibility it affords—a possibility that Badiou has carefully conceptualized. Fidelity to truth, the immortal of a resistance, militant subjectivity, the ethics of universality, and so many of his other terms, are always directed to what lies beyond the confines of mastery. Such is the revolutionary agenda of his thought.

For reasons that will hopefully become clear, Badiou has disavowed the value of semblance that I have tried to underscore. Semblance gnaws at the edges of mastery. With Badiou, what he is doing is always very real, never merely a fiction. His philosophical system seems unable to sustain itself if there is too much of this ir-reality. It is perhaps for this reason that what appeals to Badiou is not Lacan's antiphilosophy, as he calls it, nor certainly the practice of psychoanalysis, which he ignores, nor even a theory of desire, which is subsumed under other categories. Rather, it is Lacan's more systematic thought grounded in topology and mathematics.

I learned this system of his. It was an important step in learning how to rethink Lacan, to think against Adorno, to get out from the traps of nihilism and melancholia. But what once evoked enthusiasm, his belligerent rhetoric and the audacity of his formalization, left me, in the end, rather cold. It had less to do with his concepts—whose range and force of application is undeniably admirable—and everything to do with the place from which one encounters his voice. Perhaps this is the place where one would assent to Badiou, agree to follow him as master. I for one could imagine such a thing, all the while knowing that after Adorno this wasn't an open possibility for me any longer.

Badiou, one could say, is this real master that Lacan said everyone has failed to understand—the father of the primal horde. He is the one who outlines the eternal place held by the father in all his many dimensions. He is, if we are to work through a continuing *petit hysterie*, the most important figure for psychoanalysis to begin to comprehend again. The real master is the one we have to read out from Freud's myths, *Totem and Taboo (1912–1913)* and *Moses and Monotheism (1939)*—the primal father with all the women, his problematic enjoyment, the one who is always destined for murder, in which case we carry this burden of envy and guilt, narcissism and aggression.

This first appearance of the death wish directed at the father is at the foundation of our structures of kinship and community. The structure of this father is the structure that evokes a cut—the necessity of this space carved between you and you, as we saw in Hamlet. Discourse must be something held beyond each one of us, a beyond whose cutting edge becomes our saving grace. It is my hope that in this concluding section on Badiou, we will come to understand the implication of this space, no less this figure of the father.

The master is someone who we believe incarnates the exception to the rule, the first and final transgressor of the Law. As Joyce (1922/1986) humorously put it at the end of *Ulysses*, when it was a question of whether Bloom could find it in himself to be a father to Steven Dedalus:

> If he smiled why would he have smiled?
> To reflect that each one who enters imagines himself to be the first to enter whereas he is always the last term of a proceeding series even if the first term of a succeeding one, each imagining himself to be first, last, only and alone, whereas he is neither first nor only nor alone in a series originating in and repeated to infinity (p. 731).

The master is the one who imagines himself to be *first, last, only, and alone*—the beginning of the series. Is this not close to Freud's primary desire as articulated by Leclaire? Desire at its foundation and this foundational desire—as a wish to transgress, unveil, rip into, and possess—cannot be. It necessitates a cut. "I am," receives its negation, "you are not."

Badiou's smile comes to you as something that originates from himself. But even in the exchange, it always seems to return there once again. If you've ever heard him laugh it is something charming, disarming even, but it is, in its way, radically self-contained. It is different with Lacan. He initiates laughter, addresses you with it. Lacan's humorousness is something infectious. It departs from its point of origin, generates movement, and like desire tries to transcend its own boundaries only to have to begin again, which he does.

So the master's strategy is to present himself as something glorious and unpassable, and we feel him to be unassailable, an impasse. And yet, what we learn from Freud is that this identification with the master is a participation in the master's own denial. As Freud writes in *Group Psychology and the Analysis of the Ego (1921)*:

> In many individuals the separation between the ego and the ego ideal is not very far advanced; the two still coincide readily; the ego has often preserved its earlier self-complacency. The selection of the leader is very much facilitated by this circumstance. He need only possess the typical qualities of the individuals concerned in a particularly clearly marked and pure form, and need

only give an impression of the greater force and of more freedom of libido; and in that case the need for a strong chief will often meet him half-way and invest him with a predominance to which he would otherwise have had no claim. The other members of the group, whose ego ideal would not, apart from this, have become embodied in his person without some correction, are then carried away with the rest by "suggestion", that is to say, by means of identification (p. 102).

We agree, more or less, to supplement and act as his support—identifying with him, we live out a wished for mastery. We are caught like a mouse in this trap of the phallus which is the cause of the disappearance of love and desire; "the members of a group stand in need of the illusion that they are equally and justly loved by their leader; but the leader himself need love no one else, he may be of a masterly nature, absolutely narcissistic, but self-confident and independent. We know that love puts a check on narcissism, and it would be possible to show how, by operating in this way, it became a factor of civilization" (Freud, 1921, p. 93).

Where I have come to question Badiou's work is in relation to love and desire. Desire has become intrinsic to this work on the question of the life and death of psychoanalysis. Badiou, despite a trenchant Lacanianism, dislikes the category of desire. In fact he never uses it. In *Philosophy as Biography (2008),* he describes the development of his thoughts on love and desire:

> Just like everyone, in the 50s and 60s, we were tormented by sexuality …. In the end, this trouble is foreign to philosophy strictly speaking, in conformity to its great classical tradition. I would say that I learned little by little why. It is certain that sexual situations are fascinating, and it is also certain that the formalism of these situations, the erotic formalism is extraordinarily poor. And all its force depends on a repetitive injunction, with variations of little amplitude. I would say then that little by little in life a relation of charmed connivance is established with this formalism. Finally neither transgressive fascination, nor the repression of the superego, are really at their place in this affair. All that is delicious, and, after all, without great consequence for thought. I have come to conclude philosophically, that as acute as

> this pacifying charmed connivance might be, at least for me, desire
> is not a central category for philosophy, and cannot be. Or rather
> desire only touches philosophy—just as well as jouissance—as
> bodies are seized in love. That is why, from this long crossing
> through sexual torment the final result is, as I had already said for
> other reasons, that love, and not desire, must instantly return into
> the constitution of the concept (p. 15).

So while love is one of the central categories for Badiou, desire, reduced
to sexuality in its material bodily dimension, carries no traction.
Desire's formalism is poor and of little interest to Badiou and this dis-
interest of his is equated with a lack of any consequence it might hold
for thought.

The formal character of desire is siphoned into the formalism of
Lacan's mathemes and contained therein. Badiou will include psychoanalysis only under the generic truth procedure of love, one among four,
his three others being mathematics, art, and politics. What psychoanalysis proper becomes is a discourses on love that thinks the difficulty
of the two, be it the unhappy coupling of life and death drives, or man
and woman.

As much as he talked about love, mathemes, the real, Lacan is always
for me a theorist of desire; what holds the greatest traction for my work as
a psychoanalyst. Desire is never reduced to being blatantly sexual. There
was always a knot formed between, *love, desire and jouissance*. Imaginary
solutions to the complexity of this knot proliferate throughout history
from divine love to courtly love, to pornography and debasement. The
same holds just as much for the solutions offered by philosophy, which,
Lacan says, seems to search for a new ontology that is nothing short of
a question centered on being in love as the love of being.

For Freud, at the very least, the impasse is the impasse between love
and desire. Psychical impotence, for example, is a psychic division such
that "where they love they do not desire and where they desire they cannot love" (Freud, 1912, p. 183). The tendency toward debasement in the
sphere of love follows a certain logic, a special-type of object choice—the
object must be a taken one, one of ill repute, including the continuous
series of objects despite the pronouncement that their love is an event
whose "demand for fidelity" appears singular (Freud, 1910, p. 167).
In short, the object serves merely as an exchangeable prop for some
failure with respect to love and desire.

Freud says, "we have learnt from psychoanalysis in other examples that the notion of something irreplaceable, when it is active in the unconscious, frequently appears as broken up into an endless series: endless for the very reason that every surrogate nevertheless fails to provide the desired satisfaction" (Freud, 1910, p. 169). The last word for Freud is that the debasement of the love object is rather a result of an elevation of love above desire; with a wry smile Freud says that perhaps man should learn to think less highly of his wife and come to terms with the idea of incest.

The fantasy for Freud, inherent in the debasement of the object, stems from a failed prohibition with respect to incestuous desire. Desire, registered and repudiated in this way, is treated like a pollutant of the body that must be kept away from the idealized incestuous object. The decision engenders a certain logical division: there are objects which deserve to be polluted with desire on the one hand, and objects that are preserved from desire's pollutants on the other. What is preserved is a realm not necessarily for desire, but rather a realm within which to deny incestuous love.

Badiou, in seeking not only to dispense with a theory of desire, but to clear away the mistakes of philosophy—the traps it has fallen into from modernity onward—seems caught in this dilemma. It is as if philosophy must rid itself of desire. In fact, Badiou declares that he wants to depollute the body of philosophy. In psychoanalytic thought, one does not find fidelity, in Badiou's manner of defining it, without desire; and certainly not without an uncompromising work with desire in all its singular formality for a subject. I suppose for Freud and Lacan, love is only a possible horizon thereafter.

Paradoxically, quite in the spirit of Badiou, Freud said that the impasse between love and desire is our "universal affliction under civilization" (1912, p. 184). Where Freud stops short of saying anything more than this universal descriptive fact, Badiou reaches for a solution. This solution is something like a steady rearmament of philosophy with its original weapons systematic thought, a sharp line drawn between true and false philosophy. Badiou says he would like philosophy not to be so "flaccid," "defeated and limited," to stop acting like a "valet" that serves one master, for philosophy to finally quit the "self-accusatory vacillation" in the face of the crimes of the holocaust.

Like a good hysteric who loves obsessional men, his constant and rather distant labor of love grabbed my attention. If it is true that where one knows one does not enjoy, then Badiou's labor would be too much without enjoyment to be at all satisfying, precisely there where he would really have to risk his own continuity in the face of what is always going to be beyond himself. I too feel the weight of impotence, but as a psychoanalyst there is a know-how with it that doesn't translate into the kind of knowledge that Badiou seems to push for. And I think he knows this, which is why Lacan, along with psychoanalysis, drops out of the picture in his later work, relegated to the field of love.

So I wouldn't say that it was Badiou's systematizing or mathematizing that attracted me but instead his attraction to saintliness, his hatred of simulacrum. It is a fantasy of purity where the stakes of the game are this inviolate body as a body that refuses to let itself be used; the fantasy of something beyond a process of desire and signification. This inviolate body of philosophy puts the categories of language, semblance, and desire, under contestation.

This choice makes sense to me to the extent that for Lacan (1991/2007) the master always makes use of what he calls *the crystal of language*—a mythic cry embedded in the signifier at its birth. This cry mimics a kind of sufficient totality—signified like and noumenal. In using this crystal, the master tries to break with the law of the signifier, namely, the law that it always be radically independent of the signified and displaced into an endless series of which it is never its own origin. Presenting his voice as this purified cry, he makes his presence an interminable vanishing point.

So while the cry appears as "univocal," "self-identical"—it is a lie. But, it is a lie that has certain enduring effects. "Everyone jumps" when this master speaks, says Lacan, like when a baby cries or a wolf howls. As Lacan elaborated its structure, language is useful in bringing us closer to this mythical "violation of the law of the signifier," the "ultrareduced myth of being identical with one's own signifier" (Lacan, 1991/2007, p. 90). Primal repression, the divided subject, the division between word representation and thing representation, the absence of the object at the foundation of psychic reality, are all held in opposition to this myth. The myth is a myth. A cry is just another signifier.

So my rather tenacious tendency toward hysteria is most useful to me here with Badiou—locating the position of the master, locating where a discourse lapses on the question of desire. And yet, as a self-declared master one doesn't necessarily have to work so very hard. If there is an undoing, it will be his own. It will have nothing to do with others, no less myself. One cannot invest either as its support or its undoing. Neutrality demands that we, as psychoanalysts, steer clear of such tactics. While the hysteric is loath to know this—as Lacan says, she wants to be the price of his knowledge—perhaps here, for the first time I can see my own way through. The series articulated in this piece of work—Adorno, Lacan, Badiou—while ending in this figure of the master, in fact should be seen as one that is in fact set off by him.

In a strange turn, Badiou, much like Adorno, declares an end to the age of poets culminating in Celan (2005). Somewhere he must know that he is breaking this law of language, the *barre*, and preemptively, like Plato, he banishes the word. Not because of Auschwitz, as was the case with Adorno, but because the circle has been completed—from poetry to philosophy, from the presocratics to Plato, and in one more turn, from philosophy back to poetry, from Plato to Heidegger. Now philosophy must take up the reigns once again.

In praise of the poets, Badiou will say that while their project bears out a kind of truth, attempting to break through the threshold of presence, it does so only in order to orient us once more to the task of philosophy. If philosophy after Heidegger sutures itself to poetry, if philosophers from Derrida to Gadamer, and onward, relegate the project of philosophy to poetry, then to remain in this suture is a betrayal of Celan because it means that his poetry was the end of thought. Philosophy must discern its future—and it seems as if it culminates precisely in the work of Badiou himself.

With an air of justification, I can say that Badiou is, for his part, always oriented, never dislocated. He is impassable. His dream of the axiomatic principle at the heart of thought, what Lacan called Yahweh's invective ferocity, becomes the site from which he announces his sovereignty over the prostitutes of philosophy. And to the extent that this impasse also requires the exclusion of psychoanalysis—perhaps one more sophistry—his discourse depends on that which he must make his slave. Philosophy will act as no valet to psychoanalysis, no less to the poets or desire.

Badiou has been in this work from the beginning, but for me there is something in iterating this series such that now, at its end, he is a very different character then the one he was in the beginning. This isn't to say that I don't remember who he was to me then, I do, but something has changed. Is that not what we hope for when we engage in an act of writing? The encounter with Badiou is the right encounter for me at this cross roads. It is an encounter with what Lacan called *the Other side of psychoanalysis*—the discourse of the master.

A problem with truth

I would like to elaborate on what I have learned from Badiou in relation to psychoanalytic thought. Badiou's use of Lacan is important, not only for gaining some traction with Lacan, but also in thinking through the particular relationship that psychoanalysis holds with respect to truth. The question of truth strongly informs the project of Badious's philosophy, a project that can be read as a renewal of its place and prominence. Lacan, Badiou says, helps us define truth such that we can steer our way through the twin obstacles of obscurantist theories of truth and scientistic theories of truth. Badiou says, "[the] twist is not at all to put forward that the Real is unknowable, nor that it is knowable either. Lacan's thesis is that the Real has an exteriority to the antinomy between knowing and being unaware" (Badiou, 2006b, p. 3).

Badiou's work articulates this cutting edge between possibility and impossibility as occasioned by this way of rendering truth. While Badiou has a lot to say about truth, and from this we have a great deal to learn, we cannot forget the difference between the analytic position and that of the master, which turns precisely on this question of truth. What place does truth hold for us as psychoanalysts? What the master's discourse teaches us is the way in which one gets caught in this trap of truth precisely as an effect of the position one holds. If psychoanalysis does not cure through insight, knowledge, or force, how does it cure? How do we situate truth in this realm of effects that we procure?

Truth, Lacan says (1991/2007), is always to some degree impotent. It is always positioned in relationship to contingency and particularity in psychoanalysis. It gives the real back its shine, but only for a time. The radical maintenance of the place of the analyst is one where he does not get bitten by this bug of truth. Truths come—of that the analyst has had some experience—but it is not something he lays his hands on.

Rather than speaking about a doctrine of truth, psychoanalysis says something about the important relation between a subject and truth. Lacan calls this the place of the agency of a subject where truth is more than anything a relationship of cause. The meaning of the word "agent" contains the equivocation in its definition that includes the notion of being driven, being the agent *of*, being a representative or delegate of an agency. The relationship between truth and agent or agency is where I will now turn. I will do so through a reading of Badiou's work *Metapolitics* (1998/2005c). This work is essentially a critique of the concept of Human Rights and an exploration of the idea of evil that I will link back to psychoanalysis.

Under the rubric of Human Rights, Badiou shows that truth is equivalent to the capacity to determine evil *a priori*. From this definition of evil, one determines a set of laws, namely the laws of Human Rights and the threshold of their violation. Evil is determinative both of a notion of the good and of the subject. Law in this case, Badiou will say, is first of all law against evil.

For Badiou, a metaphysical notion of truth creeps back in through this door of Human Rights. In Badiou's reading, Human Rights cannot abide by a doctrine of universal truth. More egregiously, it does not ask who has the right to be the agent of truth, nor in what way, suggesting a cluster of convictions uncritically held by the ethical system of Human Rights. Badiou writes:

> We posit a general human subject, such that whatever evil befalls him is universally identifiable (even if this universality often goes by the altogether paradoxical name of "public" opinion), such that this subject is both, on the one hand, a passive, pathetic, or reflective subject—he who suffers—and, on the other, the active determining subject of judgment—he who, in identifying suffering, knows that it must be stopped by all available means (Badiou, 1998/2005c, p. 14).

Human Rights structure a conception of ethics that easily determines a course of action—a humanitarian agenda. This structure splits the field between a passive suffering subject and one who identifies and judges suffering, acting on the basis of this. Critically, Badiou states, "finally, thanks to its negative and *a priori* determination of Evil, ethics prevents itself from thinking the singularity of situations as such, which is the obligatory starting point of all properly human action" (Badiou, 1998/2005c, p. 14).

In this connection one might note that the kind of singularity that is the obligatory starting point of psychoanalysis—we must begin as if anew, each time, with each patient—is foreclosed in the *a priori* determination of evil. There is something at odds between this philosophy of Human Rights, its relationship to truth, and the conceptual system of both

Badiou and psychoanalysis. If we do not determine truth in advance, no less any conception of evil, then what can our agency be?

In the system of Human Rights, these poor, suffering, passive, victims of evil, can only identify with the power implicit in the agency of Human Rights. This figure of agency determines all the others. It is as if to say, *be strong like me, I once knew suffering but know it no longer, I will help you, I know what is right*. And yet, Badiou notes in Hegelian fashion, who is defining whom in this master-slave dialectic? Without this victim, or even without this demarcated realm of evil, Human Rights cannot define itself. Or, to put it another way, this is the logic of identification, a logic that always carves an inside edge by virtue of creating an excluded exterior.

While this is an admittedly extreme characterization, it is useful for making evident the logic of this problematic structure. The seemingly naturalized and rather conservative ethics of Human Rights, has as its counterpart a nihilistic and relativistic ethics. The latter includes, for example, the thought of Alasdair MacIntyre who famously said that the belief in Human Rights is on par with a belief in unicorns and witches. Both the absolute conviction in Human Rights and a kind of postmodern relativism fail to the extent that in the place where one solidifies truth in advance, the other equates this failure with nothingness.

Lacan is again crucial to Badiou because he represents neither of these positions at a time when these were held as the dominant paradigms. Lacan did not give up either on a concept of the subject, when this was broken apart in postmodernist theory, or a concept of truth, which was under vigorous attack as well. For Badiou, through Lacan, we find the possibility of a radical desubstantialization of truth and a subject who can seize its effects.

In analysis do we not abide by a conception of truth closer to this line of thought? The requirement of the analyst's position is such that we empty ourselves of any preconception of truth—truth always being something beyond us, articulated in a discourse that is not our own, that, if you like, belongs to the unconscious. Like Bion (1967), we are without memory and without desire. This subtractive dimension of truth is formalizable, close to Lacan's concept of the real and the crossing of fantasy.

The truths that a patient encounters are often about the effects of a supposed truth taken as substantial—for example fantasy, family mythology, identifications. These are not substantial truths, but contingent ones which define the ground of psychoanalysis starting with the impact of the accidents of life on our subjective constitution. Nowhere is this truer than in the realm of sexuality. As Jean Claude Milner (1995) powerfully renders the impact of the contingency of sexuality:

> I will advance that sexuality, in as much as psychoanalysis speaks of it, is nothing other than this: The place of infinite contingency in the body. That there is sexuation, rather than not, is contingent. That there are two sexes rather than one or many is contingent. That one is on one side or the other is contingent. That such somatic characteristics are attached to sexuation is contingent. That such cultural characteristics are attached to it is contingent. Because it is contingent, it touches infinity (cited in Johnston, 2010, p. 150)

What Milner refers to in the end with this notion of infinity can be read as universal. Psychoanalysis attends to this crossing between the particular and universal as it appears with respect to the unconscious.

On the other hand, in the logic of identification at the core of Human Rights, one has little room to be anything else beyond the preconceived categories of evil, or the figure of justice/victim of injustice. Badiou calls this the logic of the same. As he says with sarcasm, "become like me and I will respect your difference." The action is always generalizable, and your choice as a subject is to be like this, or be nothing—a perverse mirror of Lacan's ethical subject.

This is not the concept of difference as rendered by Lacan. Difference, from within this logic of the same, renders truth insignificant. There is literally an *a priori* foundation upon which anything may be discovered. For Badiou, this forbids the naming of that which, as yet, has not come to pass, namely what he calls the event. The event creates difference, it is not difference that creates the event. The question should not be about difference, but about the conditions under which a subject seizes truth through the event. "It is only through a genuine perversion, for which we will pay a terrible historical price, that we have sought to elaborate an ethics on the basis of cultural relativism. For this is to pretend that a merely contingent state of things can found a law" (Badiou, 1998/2005c, p. 28).

Human Rights is not an ethics of tolerance. It is not aimed at a tolerance of radical otherness. It is a disqualification of the Other, which, we have seen so often in modern liberal politics. It is only in relation to what is truly Other for Badiou that a new ethical relationship can be established between a subject and a world. In the words of Badiou, the system of Human Rights is a betrayal of truth. Any predetermination of the subject, let's say also of the contents of the unconscious, any prescription for how one should be in the world, is to foreclose the possibility of anything new actually emerging. In fact this kind of status quo, this normativity, is what best defines ethical systems wed to a metaphysics of evil—reified standards of one to be followed by all.

And we cannot forget the passive, pathetic, victimized subject who is at the center of this system. "At the core of the mastery internal to this ethics is always the power to decide who dies and who does not" (Badiou, 1998/2005c, p. 35). So we return once again to the problem of knowledge and mastery. Badiou's work with this problem, taken as a problem with respect to the question of truth, gives it a new characterization—the fantastic power that mastery tries to exert is always one over life and death. Unraveling the logic of identification, Badiou finds this insoluble tie between locating evil and the victim of evil in a perverse fantasy of the power to chose who lives and who dies. Become like me, or die unhappy.

I would like to elaborate this structure in relation to Freud's (1919a) work, *A Child is Being Beaten*. This fantasy, in the form of a scene where a child is beaten by a father figure, represents for Freud the scars of the Oedipus complex. This sado-masochistic fantasy powerfully induces *jouissance* or masturbatory excitement, the consequence of which is an erosion of agency and a loss of desire. In the fantasy, the self occupies multiple positions—the spectator of the beating, the aggressor, and the victim. The effect of these multiple identifications is not in the service of unraveling fantasy, but rather of sustaining it. The wish to stay a helpless child bound within the family complex, incestuous love, and the fantasy of the alleviation of guilt through punishment, circulates in this scene unbeknownst to its author.

One can identify this structure in the ethical system of Human Rights. The figure of Human Rights is the spectator of victims of evil. In positioning himself against this evil he determines his place as free of it, virtuous. In fact, this system is a system of purification, and one might speculate on the relationship between fantasy, *jouissance*, and this moral masochism. For Badiou, Human Rights is caught between these three demarcated positions.

I am slightly amused by the fact that we have come back around to the original argument concerning the seduction theory in psychoanalysis. Psychoanalysis hinges on this change from a concern with reality and veridical truth to the truth of fantasy. This change of frame provided a measure of freedom. Freud would begin to read the derivatives of the unconscious rather than seek to uncover traumatic memory. The consequence of this turn also changes the meaning of cure from one of abreaction to the subversion of a neurotic structure that often takes the form of transference to overvalued figures of authority, figures by whom, I would dare say, we wish to be beaten.

The analyst is not someone who holds a position against, before, or above such a wish. The wish is taken as universal—a scar of Oedipus. The wish, embedded in the fantasy, is unraveled in the direction of a truth that neither the analyst, nor the patient, knows in advance. The wish contains a contingent truth whose appearance is likewise characterized by some contingency. But there are, neverthless, structures that psychoanalysis formalizes—the pain of submission to life, the constraints of language and body and gender, the safety of being outside of desire, and the problems of identification with the aggressor. These act as a guide in helping a patient seize hold of their particular truth therein.

The problem of materializing or substantializing, rather than elaborating this truth can be seen in the example of Human Rights. At the very least, we begin to map the unstable identifications which force us all too fluidly to lapse between the positions of the omnipotent beating father, the victimized, beaten, but loved, child, and the "neutral" third party voyeur who cries out, "a child is being beaten!" What it is that can be found in truth that is shared universally is what defines truth as such for Badiou, for example, the impossibility of escaping the contingent effects of Oedipus on fantasy life. And yet, this universal can only be found in relation to what is most particular.

Without this ethic that aims for both absolute particularity and universality, Badiou feels we will only find a perversion of truth in the form of a disavowed attachment to the spectacle of suffering and death. As he puts it rather strongly:

> Here ethics is at the junction of two only apparently contra-
> dictory drives: since it defines Man by non-Evil, and thus by
> "happiness" and life, it is simultaneously fascinated by death
> yet incapable of inscribing it in thought. The upshot of this

compromise is the transformation of death itself into a spectacle
made as discreet as possible, a mere disappearing, regarding
which the living have the right to hope that it will not disrupt
their delusional habits of contented ignorance ... ethics oscillates
between two complementary desires: a conservative desire, seeking global recognition for the legitimacy of the order peculiar to
our "Western" position—the interweaving of an unbridled and
impassive economy with a discourse of law; and a murderous
desire that promotes and shrouds, in one and the same gesture,
an integral mastery of life—or again dooms what is to the Western
mastery of death. Against this we can set only that which is not
yet in being, but which our thought declares itself able to conceive" (Badiou, 1998/2005c, p. 36–38).

The ethics of *that which is not yet in being*, but which we can conceive,
is synonymous with Badiou's event of truth. This definition of truth
undercuts the complimentary system of a masterful desire for happiness
and resolution that lapses into a desire for death. "It is not an easy
matter to spell out the ethic of a truth: Do all that you can to persevere
in that which exceeds your perseverance. Persevere in the interruption.
Seize in your being that which has seized and broken you" (Badiou,
1993/2002, p. 47).

We persevere in the tension of desire. To my mind, the elusive
continuity provided by the unconscious and its logic can never be
entirely determined *a priori*. We have a formal knowledge of it, certainly an experience of it in a personal analysis, but in our clinical work
these only function as guidelines. The unconscious has no direct line
to consciousness, and yet some truth will manifest if we can uphold a
certain position.

At the very least, to subscribe to an ethics of the unconscious means
that we are not bearers of the law, freedom, justice, or truth. For Lacan,
the hallmark of perversion is seeing oneself as the law, as the one who
has this power of dispensation. Law and truth, exceed us, seize us,
and break us. They must always be beyond. In Badiou's words, truth
"befalls." Commitment takes the form of hope or faith that has no
representation of a future outcome (neither in the form of reward nor
punishment) and is thus the meaning of fidelity. We are not agents of
truth, rather, in relation to truth—on its path—we find our agency, our
cause. It brings us into being, if I might put it that way.

Badiou gives us back the transformative power of such categories as thought and truth, much like psychoanalysis lends transformative power to the categories of desire and speech. What Badiou posits as thinking (linking, delimiting, persevering) is close to the Freudian notion of sublimation, abstinence, and evenly suspended listening. Psychoanalysis asks that one confront the void within a given situation. There is no object of knowledge—no saving authority—that can smooth over the abyss that stands between oneself and desire.

It must be said that I find Badiou's thought useful to psychoanalysis perhaps in a broader fashion then he would ever be comfortable with. But, I'm fine with these *mere* instructions, exactly in the way that I can read Badiou's philosophical political commentary as formal instructions for thinking through the question of psychoanalysis. Through his work I can more easily grasp this cutting edge between the discourse of the analyst, the master and the hysteric. It seems to me that being used in this way should be in character with his system of thought—truths are a truth for all.

Borderlines

What if the French are right? Let us assume that I haven't drawn conclusions already. Let us assume that I am not offended as a woman by the diagnostic category of borderline psychopathology. Let us assume that I haven't found legitimacy to the feminist pleas to be spared this fate. Let us assume that I am not deeply worried about the ramifications of these ideas for the future of psychoanalysis. Let us assume that my outrage does not overshadow my attempts at clarity. Let us assume that I can believe for a minute, so as not to echo the sentiments I seek to deny, that we can have a reasonable discourse on such matters. Let us assume that I will now proceed from a point outside these two sides, to find out what it would mean if the French were right—without presuppositions. Let us assume, on one side or the other, that we feel the stakes are high. Let us assume that these assumptions are possible when we both know that they are not.

The hysteric is a relic of the early 20th century. We have the new feminine diagnosis—Borderline Personality Disorder. It is recognizable by: (1) nonspecific manifestations of Ego weakness (2) identity diffusion (3) shifts toward primary process thinking (4) primitive defenses such as splitting and denial resulting in blurring of ego boundaries such that (i) lack of the development of primary autonomy (ii) lack of anxiety tolerance (iii) excessive frustration in reality (iv) excessive aggression (5) omnipotence and devaluation of self and other (Kernberg, 1967).

From this I might recognize myself. Affirmatively I have ego strength, a coherent identity, and well functioning thought. I am reflective, integrated, bound and autonomous, and beyond this I am not only satisfied, but also capable of genuine love and empathy. To move on to the negations, I am, shall I say, not deficient, not intolerant of anxiety, not full of rage, not full of myself, not empty of myself, not needy, not desperate, not naively hopeful, and not crudely pessimistic. I am, in a word, not Borderline.

Once, a friend told me that in a meeting of some psychoanalytic association they were trying to define the difference between psychoanalysis and psychotherapy. In the end it seemed as if the only thing that determined whether one was a psychotherapist or analyst was the position of the patient, lying or sitting, in front of them. "All you have to do is look, and you can know what you are," he said to me. Perhaps it is through the Borderline that I know who I am as a psychoanalyst. And yet, by the very necessity of an external position giving me this locus internally, I am stripped of the very image and place of my authority and supposed autonomy. Is there any way around this logic of identification? Is there any way around the image taken in, the other who defines—positive or negative—in an unceasing dialectic?

The psychiatrist Otto Kernberg was one of the key figures in defining this category of the Borderline psychopathology. The Borderline's confusion of self and object land the analyst in a place where nothing new will arise except a situation such that one never seems to know who is doing what to whom. Kernberg says this with a sense of negation—the analyst should be clear on such matters. She, as he says, is out to defeat his capacity for thought.

What is interesting about this split between the one who thinks and the one who does not has everything to do with borderlines. Contemporary psychoanalysis itself is caught in an unending dispute precisely about these borderlines and the consequent split halves found in the dichotomies that define psychoanalytic groups so often these days—intrapsychic or intersubjective, repression or dissociation, the interpretation or the relationship, insight or speech. The French went so far as to say that the Borderline comes closest to the dream of psychoanalysis. She is a new mask for the question Freud brought to the surface when he drew his absolute line between consciousness and the unconscious.

It should come as no surprise that the Borderline is defined in essence by lack and excess (lack of development of primary autonomy, lack of anxiety tolerance, excess aggression, excess frustration, excess of impulse) in such a way that reproduces the very phenomenology of the drive at the cutting edge between soma and psyche. She is literally taken on the model of desire. It is not surprising that we have such trouble with her. Under the best of circumstances, this woman gives the doctor back his work as a psychoanalyst and the doctor restores to this woman her body in the form of her desire. In this, they find a dependence upon one another. To denounce one is to obliterate them both, you cannot choose which one to destroy.

Is there another way out of this fortunate or unfortunate coupling, this logic of identification? Moustapha Safouan formulates the question this way:

> The social bond consists in hatred toward the outside, is also woven on the inside out of a refusal to mourn. But to whom or to what might the mourning refer? It would be flying in the face of the evidence to answer that mourning here concerns those we have loved and lost. For the fact is that we feel such losses only too deeply. But those whom we have loved and lost are also those whom our titles to love would seem to have uncontested validity, and it is only natural that we should think to hold these titles by virtue of what we are. And yet we need to know what we are, or rather, to know the absence of what we are beyond the reference to our image (Safouan, 1993/2003, p. 67).

For Safouan the bond between the hysteric and her doctor mirrors a problematic social bond sustained with reference to an image. Because of this reliance on the image, identification in the best and worst of circumstances cannot be the path of psychoanalysis. What must be mourned is, like the case of Hamlet, beyond the reference to the image, centering more broadly on the question of crossing the castration complex. To say that there is a problem with the phallus in this couple, psychoanalyst and Borderline, is an understatement.

There is something about carving out and delineating space that haunts this dialogue about the Borderline contained in her very name. To be unborderline is, I imagine, to dream of a limitless land and to occupy that ground. The borderline, on the other hand, seems to fail to occupy any space, maddeningly liminal and evanescent. What does she want? She has all symptoms, neurotic and psychotic, which she inhabits at their border between one another. Whatever might hold beyond these two, their intractable competition for presence in an image, even in negation, is relegated to the dream of another land. What has become of our beyond? Where is the unconscious?

I am reminded of a talk I saw by a psychoanalyst who was trying to map the deficient brain of the Borderline. He glossed over it, but I caught it out of the corner of my eye—they had discovered the area of the brain associated with psychic emptiness. What a marvelous and strange idea! If you remove this part of the brain, make a hole there, what do you get? Do you get an intensification of emptiness or its relief, which would be paradoxical to say the least, if not totally absurd, such that making a hole in the brain would bring psychic fullness? The Borderline seems to throw at psychiatry the very question of presence and absence.

I had come across this a long time ago in a text by Kernberg, Seltzer, Koenigsberg, and Carr (1989). Taken from reality, no one could have written it any better. It carries within it the majesty of Beckett, actions that run through themselves with vacuity but seem necessary none-the-less, affect absent or utterly exaggerated, indifference to human difference and human difference so extreme it begs indifference, and in the last analysis, theatrical combat which persists in a form so drained and depleted one cannot help but laugh. Beckett's work is always on the borderline between comedy and tragedy.

Could we not have specified more clearly the play of the Borderline patient and her doctor? It needed its proof from the transcript:

Therapist: Well, so we are starting our psychotherapy today.
  Patient: Uh-huh.
Therapist: Is there anything on your mind?
  Patient: (long delay) No.
Therapist: I have been talking on the phone with your brother, who
             called me to tell me that you wouldn't come to the Tuesday
             session because you made a suicide attempt and were in the
             hospital … Of course this raises immediately the question

about whether you're really being able to go through this. You didn't call me …

Patient: I did call.

Therapist: You called after your brother talked with me. You told my secretary that you thought that I might be annoyed because you hadn't called …

Patient: I was very out of it (silent laugh).

Therapist: But, but you didn't really take the initiative to start out with, to let me know that you wouldn't show up at your session, at a point when you knew that—

Patient: (interrupting) can I tell you that I didn't even know what day I called. I was very out of it.

Therapist: Well, let me share with you what your brother said. He said that you had been taking some kind of medication … that's why you conveyed the impression of being out of it. Is that a fair statement?. … So I am talking about the decision you made to take those drugs.

Patient: Hmmm.

Therapist: From experience you know that once you take drugs you are out of it and you should have called me saying "I am about to take those drugs and I am not showing up on Tuesday." And you didn't do that.

Patient: It doesn't seem to me to be a normal course of procedure to call someone up and say, "I'm going to be taking an overdose."

Therapist: Well then we have to talk about this, because unfortunately that will have to be normal procedure if you want to go through with this treatment … For you to undergo this treatment, to come regularly … it is important that you take responsibility for your daily life. Otherwise you cannot commit yourself to such a treatment. So what I would like to do is to spell out what I see as a minimum requirement for our really carrying out this psychotherapy and then see what you have to say about that. OK?

Patient: If you like.

Therapist: What I would expect for you to do is whenever you feel that you are about to make such a gesture … at that point you go into a hospital immediately.

Patient: I won't go into a psychiatric hospital.

Therapist: Ok, then I won't be able to treat you. (pause) Then we have reached the end at the beginning.

Patient: You were the one that said to me that you do not feel that I would benefit from hospitalization.

Therapist: Absolutely sure, but this is not in contradiction ... certainly once you are out of control somebody has to evaluate ... and I am not going to do that.

Patient: You can't do that on an outpatient basis?

Therapist: I will not do that. Once you are in psychotherapy with me my responsibility will be to help you understand what this is all about, and the only way I can do that is by staying totally away from all the management issues regarding your suicide attempts (excerpted from Kernberg, et al., 1989, pp. 43–49).

Every time I read it, it has the same impact on me. The astonishing reversal of positions—the patient turned analyst with her, "hmmms," and finally, the kill, her "if you like," sending back the analyst's demand through his questioning "OK?" The analyst turned patient—who does all the talking and in the end must hear his own contradiction, I must not manage you, I can only manage you.

Their words circle and never meet, until, as is said, they have both reached the end in the beginning. There is no opening. There is no truth beyond the contradiction, the irrefutable gap between speaker and listener. The futility in this little transcript of a meeting is heart breaking. How does one take responsibility for their life and desire? This question is certainly the right one, but it is said in such a way that there could be no way to make contact with it as a question for oneself— its impossibility somehow rendered affirmatively. One cannot be forced to take responsibility. Responsibility cannot be structured in advance. It is dependant on an encounter with desire that is foreclosed in this account of work.

If the borderline constitutes the outside edge of identity, what is this borderline state at the periphery of the human? As the psychoanalyst, Pierre Fedida, claimed, it is precisely that—the incarnation of the inhuman, a sacrificial figure, "a female mutant Christ, whose skin is flayed in order to feel," "whose wounds are rubbed as the only condition of life in her" (Fedida, 1999, p. 64). "The Borderline state of humanity is the fulcrum at which the grimaces, simulating affects, of anonymous normality, tip over into the slow destruction of their appearances. It is also the exhaustion of the dream by the insomnia of cruelty" (Fedida, 1999). The Borderline is the line where the inhuman surfaces.

These Borderlines show not that they are Borderline but that humanity's other face is a Borderline state—tormented flesh, the disintegration of time, catastrophe that cannot be given a name or a place. If her insomnia of cruelty forces him to reproduce this dream of eradicating the borderline, his dreaming gives her the impetus to roam only in the desert of his own making. In this they sustain one another, but there is nothing admirable or new in it.

The Borderline cannot be the unsung hero I want her to be and the analyst is not the monomaniac ego, or in any case, they can be both at once not in order to break out, but to support one another in their place—to give back to one another the recognition they seek. Fragmentation or coherence—both seem to travel under the sign of the whole, the all, the one, and totality, which is as much as to say the hole, the nothing and the negative. The feminists will be angry with me, but then again I am angry with myself for having been caught in this dilemma and still having no way out. To be on one side is to find your way back onto the other, Borderline or analyst, patient or doctor, French or American.

It seems that the Borderline risks as little as her doctor in this game. She makes herself the object of dull amazement and enjoys bringing this scorn and condemnation upon herself. His failure is always not to be more amazed without, however, falling prey to this amazement. In this circle of condemnation and praise the dialogue is certainly stuck. There has to be another way out of this dilemma than what can only be seen manifestly as something disavowed, patched up, and short circuited.

If on a bad day I place myself in utmost contradistinction to my American bedfellows, disavowing everything that Kernberg stands for, his commandment is a strength in me. As Safouan puts it, "The existence of the commandment is not asserted to a lesser degree in revolt than it is in obedience. Indeed it could even be said to be more strongly asserted in revolt. For one can obey out of mere force of habit, whereas he who commits himself to an ordeal, necessarily does so under the gaze of the All-powerful" (Safouan, 1993/2003, p. 59). This is why I, at my worst and perhaps also at my best, like the analyst of borderlines and the borderline herself, amount to little more than a failed rebellion.

The analyst of Borderlines can find himself little place else than in the position of a case manager—acknowledge and practice the injunctions that I specify—which he does not wish to be. The Borderline is a purified revolt from this law in the form of a counter-identification. Borderline and analyst, whole and not-whole, phallic completeness with incompleteness as its referent, or incompleteness under the sign of the phallus—nothing more than this can be found in this field. There is no more of an elsewhere from one position to the next. The absence of what we are, or what we are in the absence of the image, is most crucial, as Safouan put it.

So the problem with the borderline as I see it is an old one. It is the same one that haunted the hysteric at the beginning of psychoanalysis—she does not create anything new. She makes present what is lost in the perspective of a fixed gaze and I wrongly assumed that that was all that could be made present. She is the appearance of disappearance itself. She is to be congratulated for such a feat! But this is not radical enough—it does not break with this virtual logic.

It is Badiou's reading of Lacan throughout his work that finally brought me to this problem of defining the cutting edge between a fundamental conservatism inherent in hysteria and what the analytic discourse aims to offer beyond this. This is the opening that is at the heart of Badiou's logic concerned with the production of something new—something that for him can only take place through a radical break. This break is equivalent to a transformation of one's subjective position in the form of love and work.

The work of Badiou's that touches this most strongly for me is a little book called *Saint Paul: The Foundation of Universalism* (1997/2003b). Badiou returns to the apostle St. Paul because for him he rigorously holds to an impossible point of truth, which he subtracts from the entirety of Christian discourse—that Christ is resurrected. For Badiou, the power of this fable, this point of the real—through which he fashions his entire discourse—clears away an imaginary consistency that surrounds Christianity, no less other religious or scientific discourses. Without this, he aims to show that one cannot found universal truth in quite the same way. Our question can be clearly formulated: What are the conditions for a universal singularity?

The Christian discourse acts like an allegory to the analytic one. In fact, Badiou is taking as his reference Lacan's theory of the four discourses (the University, the Master, the Hysteric, and the Analyst) and reconfiguring it in light of Paul (the Greek, the Jewish, the Mystic, the Christian). Christian discourse, like analytic discourse, speaks to a radical change between the subject and truth:

> Let us say that, for Paul it is a matter of investigating which law is capable of structuring a subject devoid of all identity and suspended to an event whose only "proof" lies precisely in its having been declared by a subject. What is essential for us is that this paradoxical connection between a subject without identity and a law without support provides the foundation for a universal teaching within history itself (Badiou, 1997/2003b, p. 5).

For Badiou, what Paul always reiterates is that he believes in the resurrection of Christ and that this belief, its effects, are open to all. He does not believe because, like all the other Apostles, he was there and witnessed it, nor because of fear or signs of the power of God, nor does Paul assert his belief on the basis of his own exemplary life or prophetic visions. Paul teaches only what a sense of conviction is capable of when it is founded precisely on an absence of these supports.

Greek discourse is the discourse of totality (*phusis*) and knowledge of that totality (*sophia*). Jewish discourse is a discourse of the miraculous exception to that totality—the sign, the miracle, election, and transcendence beyond the totality of this world. The mystical discourse, he says, counters both of these in their reliance on totality, being a discourse of one's ravishment by truth, here and now. It is, however, a truth that remains too private, too obscure, and tied to the hubris of personal revelation for Paul. The mystical discourse, unlike the other two, does hold an important border with Christian discourse precisely in this relation to a possible here and now encounter with truth. In fact this mystical discourse founds the possibility of Paul's encounter—his revelation on the road to Antioch.

The break that Paul makes with respect to Greek, Jewish, and mystical discourse centers on a change, as we might suspect, in relation to knowledge and mastery. A theory of salvation can be neither of these:

> Paul's project is to show that a universal logic of salvation cannot be reconciled with any law ... it is impossible that the starting point be the Whole, but just as impossible that it be an exception to the Whole ... One must proceed from the event as such, which

> is a-cosmic and illegal, refusing integration into any totality and
> signaling nothing. But preceeding from the event delivers no laws,
> no form of mastery, be it that of the wise man or the prophet. One
> may also say: Greek and Jewish discourse are both discourses of the
> Father (Badiou, 1997/2003b, p. 43).

As well, the philosopher and the prophet *know*—what is or what will
come, respectively. Paul, on the other hand, dependent on the grace of the
event, declaring an unheard, unknown, and unseen possibility, "properly
speaking knows nothing .... According to the truth of a declaration
and its consequences, which being without proof or visibility, emerges
at that point where knowledge, be it empirical or conceptual, breaks
down" (Badiou, 1997/2003b, p. 45).

What the Christian discourse names is both the division of the subject
and the possibility of its overcoming in an act of faith, love, and declaration. The subject that has "exited from unity," that is fallen, is cleft by
a separation between law and sin, life and death, doing and thinking.
Only this pure act, this leap, can create a point of radical subjectivity:

> Let us generalize a little. For Paul, the man of the law is one in
> whom doing is separated from thinking. Such is the consequence of
> seduction by commandment. The figure of this subject, wherein the
> division lies between a dead Self and the involuntary automation
> of living desire, is, for thought, a figure of powerlessness. Basically,
> sin is not so much a fault as living thought's inability to prescribe
> action. Under the effect of the law, thought disintegrates into pow-
> erlessness and endless cogitation because the subject (the dead Self)
> is disconnected from a limitless power: that of desire's living auto-
> mation (Badiou, 1997/2003b, p. 83).

This is, quite simply, the problem of the unconscious. This is the problem of being alienated from our desire. The resurrection in Paul, for
Badiou, radically redistributes life and death back to their proper place.
That is its grace. It is the grace, from my perspective, that comes of
reclaiming one's desire.

In Paul, Badiou says, truth is literally subtracted and extracted out
from the power of death—not in its negation or glorification, but in and
through affirmation. This affirmation, coming from what is essentially
negative, eradicates the problematic effects of negativity for the subject.

Death is retroactively identified as a path, not a state of things. Death is not simply what is, but is rather something closer to a choice, and an ethical choice surrounding what it is that "filliates us," what "suspends difference"—namely, what is universal (Badiou, 1997/2003b, p. 73).

Universal truth subverts an old law that divided the subject and divides subjects—my unknown sin in me, your unknown sin in you. For Badiou, the power of this event has nothing whatsoever to do with opinion. It traverses opinion—avoids it ultimately through its foundation in universality. It is born in weakness and is tied to an act of continual labor—what Paul calls hope, fidelity, and love:

> The declaration will have no other force than the one it declares and will not presume to convince through the apparel of prophetic reckoning, of the miraculous exception, or the ineffable personal revelation. It is not the singularity of the subject that validates what the subject says; it is what he says that founds the singularity of the subject … it must be borne humbly, with a precariousness appropriate to it … [it] must be accomplished in weakness for therein lies its strength. It shall be neither logos, nor sign, nor ravishment by the unutterable (Badiou, 1997/2003b, p. 54).

We renounce the push toward transcendence and instead encounter what the resurrection represents and offers in the form of the immanentization of spirit. The subject is transformed through his faith and this renewal lies in being traversed by this infinite power of truth.

There is something important for psychoanalysis in Badiou's St. Paul, especially when it comes to a question of life and death, of courage and fidelity, and also about the handling of truth: "thus, one may justifiably say that he bears it only in an earthen vessel, day after day enduring the imperative—the delicacy and subtle thought—to ensure that nothing shatters it. For with the vessel, and with the dissipation into smoke of the treasure it contains, it is he, the subject, anonymous bearer, the herald, who is equally shattered" (Badiou, 1997/2003b, p. 54). Whether we always, eventually, succumb to this shattering, is perhaps more of an analytic truth than a Badiouian one. Nonetheless, this precarious action and the emphasis on the delicacy of thought, is close to the work of psychoanalysts day after day.

St. Paul is a parable of the affirmative power of desire. When it is repressed, caught in the network of the death drive, its effects are essentially negative. For Badiou, when a subject is put in relation to this unknown, this is not only revolutionary, but a fundamentally ethical stance. By Badiou's logic then, it matters not that he is French, nor that I am American, neither that he is a philosopher, nor that I am a psychoanalyst. This argument is rendered inconsequential since, if I am to speak, it is not from any given substantial position, from any objective aggregate.

Badiou redescribes the logic of the event through this reading of St. Paul, which he calls the grace of the new. In psychoanalysis, the declaration of the existence of the unconscious is close to the event of truth, for Paul, the truth of the resurrection.

What is left for psychoanalysis in its work with this ineffable thing—the *unbewust*? To declare that the unconscious exists, without righteousness or justification, is an inherently weak position that we must bear out, by Badiou's logic, if our discipline is to have any effect of truth:

> [It confounds] those who "when they measure themselves by one another and compare themselves with one another, are without understanding", ascribes no redemptive signification to the apostle's tribulations. Here again, as always, it is a question of the earthen vessel, of the post-eventual bearing of weakness, of the destitution of worldly criteria of glory: "if I must glory, I will glory in the things that show my weakness"(Badiou, 1997/2003b, p. 104).

The French are right then, to answer the question with which we began, to the extent that they do not redeem the Borderline, but redeem neither the borderline nor the analyst of borderlines, nor do they condemn them either.

The Borderline is she who holds up the mirror as the reverse side of the face—death. The analyst of Borderlines submits to the reflection and embodies a dead law whose extolled virtue is supposed to give life. The unconscious, as an event that the two share, is eradicated from their relationship as that universal which exceeds them. In fact, again and again we are told to have no faith in her unconscious and a total mastery of our own. Theory states that we should have no faith in what she comes to say to us as a psychoanalyst—it is blind primary process, her *as if* personality, evacuation, concreteness, a whole host of non-specific manifestations of ego-weakness. In short, detestable weakness. Countering it with strength means analysis has to go down the path of arm-wrestling the Borderline out of helplessness.

Hearing Badiou, I say: "Do not work from within her gaze and her weakness will be transformed, which is as much to say that our weakness is transformative." Such will have been the analyst's fidelity to the unconscious, our uninterrupted labor to remain in fidelity to a truth that can only be born in weakness. This fidelity to the unconscious seems to me to define what it is to be an analyst. I am in Badiou's debt. Through him, I know more of what kind of analyst I would like to be. I am the one in the process of vanishing, not to lapse into the borderline, the attractive immanence of her truth, but in order locate the borderline position of the analyst.

On love and shame

So it is as a clinical psychoanalyst that I must return to Badiou. It is from a very different place than that in which his philosophy is articulated. There is trouble. Psychoanalysis has maintained a kind of self-imposed exile from academia—at its most extreme here in America—with fewer and fewer clinical analysts that aim to speak outside of their institutes and enclaves as clinical analysts. But in the end I must try.

The great contradiction in addressing this to Alain Badiou can be seen in what he told me once—that he wished to know nothing about psychoanalysis and that if I liked I could call this his symptom. How do I understand these words from my master? I don't think he's alone in not wanting to know anything about psychoanalysis. Oddly, psychoanalysts themselves seem to display this tendency through their own withdrawal.

But what do we make of this decision? Badiou is a philosopher who considers Lacan his event. He is, as he has said, a great "Lacanian." But then we have to take account of the fact that Lacan was first and foremost a psychoanalyst, with a practice and a discourse that was meant to speak to analysts about analysis. I think we all too easily forget this in this age of cultural criticism. And do we not then fall into the trappings of a symptom when we promote this wholesale repression? A passion for ignorance—as is the case with symptoms.

Like symptoms themselves, psychoanalysis is, in Badiou's system, everywhere and nowhere. One can read from this a structure—it is centered around a hole, but one which has come to be filled with a little symptom that cannot be known, cannot be spoken. For Badiou, psychoanalysis is a part of the truth procedure of love but not equivalent to it, is taken up in Lacanian structures that inform him, has some bearing on a theory of the subject, and yet, the clinical dimension is dismissed, because truth for Badiou, should always be free. Perhaps it can be subsumed under some idea of an antiphilosophy, but, in the end, the final word is that it cannot, and should not, be confused with philosophy. Mums the word, while that was, I'm sure, a mouthful.

But let us try to seriously consider the question of the relationship between philosophy and psychoanalysis (lest we lapse into mere cultural criticism once again). I often think of philosophers like Derrida or Deleuze, or even Žižek, for whom a concern with psychoanalysis is central. Their discourse was a perpetual game of Fort-Da, and, for my part, I recognize little in them that resonates with what I do as a practicing analyst. Ironically, Badiou is something else entirely: he is the one philosopher who has chosen to disavow this confrontation with psychoanalysis. It is a fascinating sacrifice of knowledge with respect to psychoanalysis. Perhaps, we might speculate, that it engenders an effect of truth in relation to it.

Here I speak as a psychoanalyst who takes Badiou at his word. He determined a large part of my formation, as we call it, as an analyst. His discourse had a profound effect on my reading of Lacan, and it led me back to a particular strain of his thought, in particular on the question of modesty. This is perhaps not an obvious point, even if it has become all too obvious to me. I forget the clichés that subsume Lacan. The violence he still provokes. Perhaps the glare coming off of so many Lacanian objects—the jargon, mathemes, formulae, graphs—prevents one from seeing this other side of Lacan. I see in him a modest analyst, in love with madness, feminine madness in particular, but through a real sense of limitation, not in the sense of a discourse on finitude, but that which comes from understanding what it means to be an analyst, to act from that impossible place. Badiou, for me, reads Lacan here.

All that blather of Lacan's about the analyst playing dead, playing dumb, allowing himself to be a dupe, and love the unconscious, becoming, as he says, as stupid as a cabbage. Certainly, if a symptom is a passion for ignorance, the analyst professing to be a lively and knowledgeable fellow would get nowhere. As Badiou says, impossibility has to delimit the conditions of possibility. Or further, this is the very "power of the impossibles." For Lacan, to be an analyst means learning to live through the vertigo of the analytic position, being put in the position of supposed knowledge and having to find the way both to accept that position and yet internally to refuse it. One also must find the way to allow oneself to be discarded, in the end, by another.

At that juncture, I am forced to confront a divide at the place of this symptom of Badiou's, as he calls it, where I can no longer locate my place in his discourse for the reason that there is a difference between a discourse on modesty and a modest discourse. It is to the latter that this work was always aimed no matter how often it failed, no matter how often my voice failed. I could have taken up a position of mastery, even as I eschewed knowledge. It would have made writing much easier. I have tried something else. I have wrapped this work in a conceit of dreams.

So let me tell you, once again, about a dream. This one, unlike the others, is entirely populated, but once again there is something of locating a certain kind of object. I walk into a library to look for my husband, but I do so by looking for another man, a philosophy professor of mine who is, in fact, dying. It is a disorienting and strange tactic, no doubt, but who am I to argue with the logic of dreams. A third man, who I will find out later is a visiting professor, asks me if I am just going to stand there with my mouth agape. I am enraged and humiliated, and a sense of shame, like finding yourself naked in public, overwhelms and paralyzes me. I almost apologize and give way to inhibition. Instead I find myself saying, "I find my way by looking for the man who I know will never be there." The word left in my mouth when I awoke, was not in fact "agape" but Agape—Christian Love of thy neighbor.

Certainly, one can glean a certain hysteria in this, an old and not so trustworthy friend. She usually leads me astray, except, of course, when it comes to a certain question of truth. Lacan, famously said that if there is anything the hysteric loves, it is truth, and she brings one into question precisely there. She raises the value of the symptom to the level of truth, which, as he says, is always the truth that the master is castrated.

The difficulty with hysterics is that they never lay a hand on truth, and, as it goes, she usually winds up with precisely what she claimed not to be looking for (as it is said a master). So, perhaps, knowing a certain inclination I have that is particularly hard to escape, I reverse strategies, and find exactly what I want, precisely by looking for something else.

This something else—in the case of the dream a someone else—that will never be in his place, means one can find the right place, at the right time. It is about a stance that one occupies as a matter of tact. There are four figures in this dream: myself, and three men—the interlocutor, my husband (whom I presumably find), and the absent one.

Lacan states that for the hysteric, it is only if things are well with the God who is dead, who is not there, that she can do anything with a real man. Otherwise, we run into the perennial problem of the love of a hysteric that flows in the beauty of a virile identification, the "implacable erotic transference" as Badiou calls it (Badiou, 1998/2005b, p. 53).

And in the case of my interlocutor, he is that figure Lacan called the non-dupe-err, the one who refuses to make a mistake and so goes astray. For this figure, the God who is dead is clearly not dead enough and the indictment of what should be done properly in libraries, rather than standing around with our jaws dropped, mouths wide open, shows that he is up to his ears in a shame before this God, with which he can do little else than dump it onto his neighbor. I could have crawled off in the face of him. We are sometimes at our best in dreams.

And, of course, there is this question of the living husband and the absent man. One of the thoughts I had upon awakening was that it is impossible to look for someone. The more you look for the signifiers you expect to see, the more you are led astray. At least for me, the moment that I drop the intensity of my gaze, I suddenly allow some new sign into consciousness that allows me to find what I am seeking. In a crowd, for example, I look for some obvious sign—my husband's bald head, his interminably black shirts—and not until I stop looking do I find what will actually let me locate him— the slouch in his shoulders, his particular gait, a thickness of neck.

This is a description of the tact of the analyst. The stupidity and possibility of surprise allows one to find her way to speech; it opens up a space, a gap. Without this gap? Without the man who will never be in his place? There are a thousand ways one goes astray between the beginning and the end of analysis, in the space between "agape" and Agape (with the embarrassing allusion I cannot help but hear—from the oral dimension to sublimation proper).

For Lacan, one of the signs that one is approaching this hole, this gap, is not in fact Love, but shame. It is only through shame that we pass toward a doing well with a "God who is Dead." The dilemma here is close to what we already mentioned as the impossible choice of modernity for Badiou—the inability to chose between mastery and truth. Badiou would prefer that "truth be articulated onto the void," to "discover a thinking of choice and of the decision that would go from void to truth without passing through the figure of the master" who is either, invoked again and again, by said visiting professors, or sacrificed, in the "immanence and immobility" of a hysterical terror (Badiou, 1998/2005b, p. 53–54).

Lacan took from Hegel the link between the death of God and love of one's neighbor. The destruction of the law into the pure formality of Agape—the maxim to "love thy neighbor as thyself"—contains the risk of going to the heart of a necessary emptiness. For Hegel, what dies on the cross is not a finite representative of God, but the God beyond himself. Man stands alone in the face of the Other who becomes an abyss. It is only this structure that allows us to truly love in that uniquely Christian sense, from that edge.

This is how Lacan understands the problem of sublimation. The good is sacrificed in the name of desire, because what one comes to know is that desire is always sacrificed in the name of a good. The good, even when it is the love of a spouse, makes that other a counterpart to the detriment of a sublimation that must attempt to recoup it otherwise.

In his book on St. Paul, Badiou (1997/2003b) shows how the Christian discourse is itself an articulation based on a man who is not there or never will be in his place (dare I say the empty tomb) and Agape. The impossible (as a belief in the resurrection) is what gives strength to the place of the Pauline discourse. Love in Paul, says Badiou, is the affirmation of the labor of truth, the power of thought in a universal declaration that cuts unilaterally. But we cannot forget that this declaration, this mighty affirmation, comes from a point of near impossibility and radical emptiness.

What I would like to say about Badiou touches upon this scene in the library. It is about the stance that one occupies in relation to shame, modest discourse, and this symptomatic ignoring of psychoanalysis. Where in Badiou does this symptom of psychoanalysis rear its head? I would like to say in the absence of shame, a certain fatigue with the attempt to master everything, and the only place where a law is articulated in the name of a good—the idea he has of the good of philosophy, its separation in function from the truth procedures. Badiou, I think, loves philosophy very much. But it is possible to love too much. Psychoanalysts have learned that hysterical ideals with respect to love are always at the heart of symptoms. One runs into trouble again. Love as labor means love comes later, like an aftertaste left in one's mouth.

Lacan reminds us of this phenomenon, referring to a peculiar fact we see endlessly in our offices: what if, for the sake of your wife's happiness, you sacrifice your own—only to find that hers will vanish before your eyes? "Enjoy with the wife you love" is indeed the height of this paradox, because it is precisely loving her that creates the obstacle (Lacan, 1991/2007, p. 190). Rather than take this direct path of love, Lacan suggested we approach it from another angle, that we go in the direction of shame.

Do a bit of analysis, Lacan says, and you will see that you already have enough shame "to open a shop" (Lacan, 1991/2007, p. 182). This was brought up in the context of the events of May 1968, when Lacan said that what the revolutionaries did not understand was precisely this shame, the system that produced the immense shame of living. In the name of the shame of others, they took to the streets as if they were out from under it themselves. "You cannot get out without entering," he cautioned them, and further, "What you aspire to as revolutionaries is a master. You will get one" (Lacan, 1991/2007, p. 207).

As analysts, the use we can make of shame is the only bit of tact left to us with the symptoms of our time. For Lacan, as we said, there is only one virtue: modesty, *pudeur*. He writes that "it is impossible for the honest to die of shame. … You know … that this means the real. … If it happens now, well then, it was the only way to deserve it …. You were lucky." Otherwise you do not die and you are left with a life of it "by the bucketful by virtue of the fact that it's not worth dying for." This, he says, is what "psychoanalysis discovers" (Lacan, 1991/2007, pp. 181–182).

The closer one gets to shame, the closer one is to the hole in the real from which a new truth might arise. We must get as close as we can to this hole if we want anything to do with the subversion, or even just the rotation, of the master's discourse where everyone is sold short on love. What is the problem with the master? It is a real master that Lacan says everyone forgets, especially in a hysteria that casts him as a sort-of tyrant.

Like Freud, Lacan was at times seemingly no friend of the philosophers. In the 1968 seminar, he says, "Philosophy in its historical function is this extraction, I would almost say this betrayal, of the slave's knowledge, in order to obtain its transmutation into the master's knowledge" (Lacan, 1991/2007, p. 22) Moreover, he asks, "Does the master who brings about this operation of displacing, the conveyancing, of the slave's knowledge want to know?" His answer, "A real master … doesn't desire to know anything at all—he desires only that things work" (Lacan, 1991/2007, p. 24). One might add: that work militantly at that.

This master, Lacan says, is, like the benevolence and love of most Fathers, thoroughly castrated. It is this position which makes his discourse so unassailable. It is for this reason, this structure, that the tools of the analyst are the power of the impossibles. We learned this from Dora, who gave the key to Freud in the very discovery of her transference (our greatest resistance and our greatest ally).

So what is it about these fathers that their daughters find so hard to know? It is that they want to make too many women happy, all the women (and then the whole world to boot), to be precise. Think of all the jewelry Dora's father had to buy for his wife, his lover, his daughter, and the cases to enclose them as well. And, as captains of industry, they feel it their duty to get the whole world up and running, which is, to their great shame, impossible. Impossibility wears them down and tires them out. This father does nothing more nor less than occupy the contradictory place of not knowing what he wants and always ending up at some distance from it—the women and his work. On the other hand and on the other side, "being deprived of woman—this, expressed in terms of the failure of discourse, is what castration means" (Lacan, 1991/2007, p. 154).

Shame, when working on that side of the truth of desire in analytic work, holds up the power of the impossibles rather than grinding away in the face of them. This edge of impossibility, and the shame at the sham of what one does, are the only ways I can work clinically. Orienting oneself, knowing how to find one's way, is different from what one may call the register of having—possessions, accumulation—and this holds just as much for truth itself. Something must be done with the philosopher's truth, because in and of itself, it is a trap. As Lacan writes, "One doesn't marry truth; there can be no contract with her, and even less can there be any open liaison. She won't stand for any of that" (Lacan, 1991/2007, pp. 184–185).

Lacan said that the analyst is the one who "leaves the thread of … truth to the one who already has his worries with it" (Lacan, 1991/2007, p. 186). He will have to worry about it like a curse and go to work. In the end, the function of this curse of truth is a "collapse of knowledge" which holds up certain self-fashioned laws. I hear such a curse in the "why" of my interlocutor in the dream, the visiting professor in the library.

Lacan continues, if many believe that I am in possession of truth, or have begun to worry about it, they say, as a result of me, "it's through not giving the appearance of having laid a finger on it" (Lacan, 1991/2007, p. 185). This act of refusal in the position one holds, which one might imagine as a form of exclusion, is actually the only path toward collaboration. This is why it is at the foundation of the analytic act. If you want subversion, you have to love the impossibility, the shame, of never being able to die from impossibility or shame. It provides you with that mysterious thing called "tact" that gets things moving—not too much, not too little.

One might ask: Isn't it modest to take away from the philosopher, in the very field in which he works, his being able to produce a truth himself? Does Badiou not say that philosophy limps behind its four truth procedures? The false modesty of a symptom is cunning. Here philosophy oscillates symptomatically between being an exalted and depraved figure much like the hysteric herself and the father whom she simultaneously tears off the pedestal only to seat him there once again.

Let me say then that this separation between philosophy and psychoanalysis, this separation between the gathering of the conditions of truth and those four little discourses that go to work for the great father, is also (for better or worse) impossible. For me, it is a matter of understanding what to do, tactfully, with this impossibility. I do not propose to have an answer as to the similarity or difference between psychoanalysis and philosophy except to begin to address it through the division Badiou makes and the strange place to which he has relegated clinical psychoanalysis. The minimal difference manifests itself in relation to shame. It is only this that holds the limit. The master has none, the university has too much, the hysteric speaks its truth only in her symptom, and an analyst finally makes do with its impossibility.

The system, Lacan says, despite producing the immensity of the shame of living, "has no shame … . This translates as—it's impudence" (Lacan, 1991/2007, p. 190). So it would do one well not to go in that direction. It is here that one finds the only law that could be taken as moral in Lacan. Thievery, tyranny of knowledge, forcing truth, are only of the order of the structures of discourse—they are impossible by virtue of the fact of being structures of discourse but, as such, are unavoidable and so cannot be taken morally. They are always at work. If one allows this shame its place, she will allow herself to slip between these structures of discourse—to find her way toward tact; she will be able, in Badiouian fashion, to "labor under truth, labor as love" (Badiou,

1993/2003b, p. 96) But here, then, there cannot be a neat division. We have to slip in the vertigo of this impossibility. Our discourse must bear the trace of this shame.

No one comes to know shame better than the analysand in the encounter with an analyst. Perhaps one experiences shame only in the face of an analyst these days for one particular reason—he represents the consolidation of the law in the supposed subject of knowledge. One goes for no other reason. Even miraculously, if one is aware of that fact. And one might say about Badiou that he wants to know nothing of psychoanalysis to the extent that his desire is that philosophy gets back to work on the level of truth. And yet we find in this desire an underlying love of truth, and, like the hysteric, a centering of discourse around a kernel of symptomatic refusal.

Symptoms attest to that divide between thinking and doing, between mastery and truth, which leaves psychoanalysis in a domain where insight is valued over speech, which, in effect, changes nothing for a subject in relation to mastery. Philosophy, in this same vein, can speak about modesty but never from within a position of modesty—which, ultimately, I think, is the lesson of Badiou's work, even the heart of his revolutionary politics. As a philosopher, Badiou does not create, he merely gathers, and if this is not the thievery of the master, then perhaps it is too much like the discourse of the university and the gathering of knowledge, the systematizing of truth—another trap of desire in any case. None of this discussion would stand as a condemnation to the extent that we no longer take any of this to be anything other than the permutations of discourse (impossibility).

But not to condemn brings into question one's relation to shame. If there is glory to be had it is more certainly to be had as a philosopher than as a psychoanalyst. We have long since left the best-sellers list. That doesn't mean that I do not procure as an analyst a certain force of intrigue. It may be my only cache. But it is precisely here that I can think of little else than shame. That is my experience.

The proletariat can be redeemed, as can the professor. Also woman, at times, in her particular elevation. Even our elusive master, who tires when he tries to make the whole world happy. But what does the analyst do? Whatever it is, it is clearly absurd, making himself the cause of desire, of what Lacan will call the insane operation of a psychoanalysis. The shame I experience after sessions pivots between "what have I done" and "why, in God's name, did that work?" Perhaps analysis takes this shame to its limit. Badiou was one of those who taught me—strength in "weakness," not a weakness made strong.

If any academic with a penchant for radical leftist ideology feels shame at the abstraction of his work, psychoanalyzing takes this abstraction beyond any point of recognition, into pure semblance. It may be this that holds as the subversive power of the analytic discourse. If the hysteric ends in a deprivation worn on one's sleeve and takes off running around the streets, the analyst does nothing but sit. Knowledge does not progress through critique or filter or force but through an audacious leap through artifice in which we give truth back to God. The analyst's atheism is a strange one—shameful, really.

As Joyce said to Nora, in love letters that show the power of wrestling with one's relation to shame, "I gave others my pride and joy. To you I give my sin, my folly, my weakness and my sadness" (Joyce, 1966, p. 107).

But there's the rub. Badiou encountered an analyst about whose work he says he wants to know nothing. I think, in the end, that is right. I would say that his encounter allowed him to function in the place of a master signifier. His is a new discourse, in that it is an audacious leap through artifice. If psychoanalysts do not any longer know of this master's discourse, then it is clear that we need Badiou, that I needed Badiou, and that philosophy needs Badiou. To the extent that his philosophy, separated out from psychoanalysis through the force of a particular kind of ignoring, makes one ill at ease and yet gets one to work, there is no harm, merely shame. It cannot be transgressed, not on one side or the other. All that one has left is to wait for the fall. If it is not Badiou who disappears at this point, then it is I.

The leap through artifice requires that we give truth back to God. I give truth back to the philosophers. I give truth back to Alain Badiou.

To end by quoting Badiou himself on Beckett: "It will always be a question of making sense of the magnificent formula from *The Unnamable* (1953/2006): 'I alone am man and all the rest divine ...' To relegate the divine and its curse to the periphery of saying, and to declare man naked, without either hope or hopelessness, relentless, surviving, and consigned to the excessive language of his desire" (Badiou, 2003a, p. 117).

Lacan, like me, speaks alone as a psychoanalyst. To do so is the only fragile and risky guarantee that we have to give, which is essentially nothing. As Lacan said, Love is to give what one does not have. What bearing does this have for the philosopher? Like a good analyst, I will end provocatively by saying nothing at all.

CHAPTER FOUR

Last remarks

Leclaire's notion that there is no truth beyond or before unconscious desire, which supports truth as much as it veils it, is the premise on which this work has been written. Like Alain's three second book, likened to the three second session, it both supports his truth, that of the formalization of philosophy, along with his desire for the absolute formula to be synonymous with himself. It also veils his desire that this formula eclipse desire which cannot but extend itself, in particular, to the sacrifice of psychoanalysis. He would like to eradicate psychoanalysis from his knowledge. Perhaps it means he breaks free of his debt to Lacan, just as Freud's book of dreams was the beginning of the dissolution of his tie to Fliess, which ended, as we might remember, in his failing to give him credit for the theory of bisexuality.

In any case, this fact about unconscious desire, in the end, has nothing to do with me or with Badiou. I can only offer the semblance of an instruction, which is the closest I have gotten to any formula. As for psychoanalysis I learned from Badiou what I have come to see as our only fighting chance—to remain in complete fidelity to desire, to the unconscious—the militant maintenance of a strength to stand there when "nothing is promised to us but the power to remain true to what comes to us" (Badiou, 1998/2006a, p. 23), even if that is nothing.

135

As these dreams progressed, from the first to the third, I had the strange sensation of being able to write less and less about them as if one was closer to this supposed formula of desire—the place where interpretation stops, the moment when an object comes closest to the thing and no longer requires the supplementation of a meaning. A purified signifier, close to absolute nonsense, impossibility, and something like the rhythm of the body that animates speech.

What does this mean for writing? It is surely different from Badiou's infinite production of texts, out from under the "truth" that he has grasped. His work, as he likes to tell us, is planetary. He is "living in thought like someone who had fallen upon an oil well: an inexhaustible intellectual energy lay at my disposal" (Badiou, 1998/2006a, p. iv). A truth, Badiou has said, is "scarcely-said," and yet, miraculously, he finds a great deal to say about it. For Lacan, the ethics of the analyst is quite different than this. Lacan asks:

> what sort of disaster does analytic knowledge produce? That is what was in question, what has been in question for as long as it has not made them all itching to become authors. It is a very curious thing that the non-signed [anonymous authors] should appear paradoxical, whereas of course over the centuries all the honest men there have been have always acted as if someone had torn their manuscript from their hands, as if someone played a dirty trick on them. No one expected to be sent a note of congratulations on publication" (Lacan, 1991/2007, p. 191).

The anonymity for Lacan was important, and in a way, these dreams grew increasingly anonymous. This also holds true for our three figures. Even further, this makes the task of writing increasingly difficult, also meaning that in order to do so one had to start taking risks, forcing a measure of sacrifice. Anonymity might be the cover that allows the work to be *ripped* from one's hands, to bare a certain amount of shame.

Badiou will say about anonymity that "ethics … consists entirely in exercising a sort of restraint with regard to its powers … the reserve of the non-saying; in the limit of the voice vis-à-vis that which shows itself; in that which is subtracted from the absolute imperative to speak the truth" (Badiou, 2004, p. 116). This quality of reserve came to guide my idea of the ethics of psychoanalysis precisely as prudence, tact, grace, and modesty, which were only possible as linked to the feminine. This was done in accordance with the Lacanian collapse of the feminine and the unconscious—the necessity for a confrontation with impossibility.

It took my finding my way out from under Adorno's seductive weight, out from under the betrayal of Lacanians, and with Badiou, it was a relationship such that his inability to subtract himself from his discourse meant that I must go to the very edge of my own precisely in order to uphold it. If I hadn't grasped this possibility before I entered into his thought, I certainly have an indication of it now. Like this work, it is only through a series that is set off, Adorno, Lacan, Badiou that one can discover what belongs to them—that one can discover what it is to be given back their desire.

So I have tried and most likely failed to write this kind of ethics in setting off this series. It is a task slightly different from any writing *about* ethics, and tries to remain closer to desire pure and simple. It has meant, I'm sure, that my passion has gotten the best of me, which will no doubt turn-off a great many of you. I will try and take it as a compliment, as did Lacan, since the attempt to invoke desire might mean an inspiration toward judgment. Impetuousness has more possibility than the supposed lack of it.

Psychoanalysis, one could say, if it does anything, truly initiates a series, a chain of associations, a set of signifiers, which begin to articulate desire. This is why movement is so important. One could say that is all that psychoanalysis does—it gets things moving. It is around these figures that it begins to highlight the subject; figures which no doubt condense with the analyst him or herself on whom its final act will turn. By virtue of this it gives rise to a singularity, not of the others, but of the subject. It produces a subject in rendering this other utterly anonymous, nameless even. Not my father, not my mother, not my maternal grandmother, not Adorno, not Lacan, not Badiou. But not nothing either.

These others who had paralyzed the subject with their imagined watchful gaze, return to the mere fact of an encounter. Someone I came to love and came to leave. It happened, that's about all that needs to be said; and it has its effects, structural ones in fact, which was what I was after from the beginning. The slow rate of change. This is Lacan's definition of truth—universal in structure, singular in content; and the formula as formula with the particular words and images that decipher it. It constitutes a psychoanalysis oriented toward the future, and by virtue of this may be the sole means for addressing its life and death. With the past relegated to the past, what matters is what is said.

This changes, as Lacan said in *Television* (1974/1990), the Kantian question "what may I hope for?" (which already shows that the addressee is to provide an answer in the form of an object) to "from where do you hope?" "From where do you hope" reorients the subject as a question, as someone in the midst of a search already bound by desire. So truth be told, a great deal of this work is wrapped in a complete conceit—the future of psychoanalysis and my dreams? Are you joking? Why does it matter that psychoanalysis disappoints you and whether or not you get out from under that? That you hope for too much? With a grandiosity you'll no doubt fail not to detect, I suppose with Freud I must ask the reader "to make my interests his for quite a while, and to plunge with me, into the minutest details of my life" (Freud, 1900, p. 121). I will, with a lingering tinge of hysteria, take the life and death of psychoanalysis as my own.

Badiou wrote that "what [truths] produce (the unnamable in language itself, the potency of the pure letter, general will as the anonymous force of every namable will, and the Two of the sexes as what has never been counted as one) in variable situation is never but a truth of these situations … onto which no knowledge can 'pin' its name, or discern beforehand its status" (Badiou, 1989/1999, p. 107). So the situation was my own, it was the time I had spent with psychoanalysis as a discipline in various contexts, it was my educational experience, it was, of course, my analysis, and it was these dreams. Is it too much to say that each dream falls into these effects of the truth of a situation—the unnamable in the memorial, the letter, the general will that fells, and the one that is never counted, the always absent one?

If it is only there where I am not that I am thinking, then dreams are one place that we can think in the place of nonknowledge, a raid on the inarticulate that had to be my own. I took the risk of bringing this into articulation through the series of transferences—Adorno, Lacan, Badiou. Dreams, it is said, take hold when a transference is at work, "raising the question of the secret of phantasy … the profound passion that drives the discoverer of enigmas and the explorer of origins … manifest at once in the intensity of the transference" (Leclaire, 1968/1998b, p. 62). These two, dreams and transference, taken together, point to a writing that complicates the process of exchange, destroys any supposed symmetry between the partners, and in this, risks losing them completely. It does so founded on little else than a guiding ethics and an intensity of passion. It aims for a fundamental change in the nature of discourse. Whether that happens is not up to me anymore. You will read this as you choose.

With every one of these thinkers there was for me in the beginning a kind of madness, reading for hours on end, I couldn't get inside it enough, much like the beginning of any common love affair. I used to, I'm sure you can imagine, become increasingly disappointed. The reading would trail off with a mild depression. It isn't like that so much for me anymore. It's more like enthusiastically waiting to be inspired again, perhaps with an anxiety that the last may truly be the last. A change of discourse is indicated by Lacan when something has fallen. Love is in the air. A turning has initiated a delicate but powerful chain of events that cannot be stopped, that one would never let stop. It is there that it becomes a matter of life and death.

In the final editing of this piece of work I had a dream I think, perhaps, in order to finally close it. I was on a train with someone who is of immense importance to me and also to this piece of work. The train is strewn with objects whose quality as object comes across very clearly somehow—they seem to have no utility whatsoever. They are almost like objects purified as things. One of the objects starts screeching. He picks it up, takes out a screw-driver, and makes a quarter turn in a switch on the back. He looks at me and says, "some of them are made for that, you just might not necessarily know it." It returned to its status as thing.

I think I could properly say that this is the formula for my desire—the importance of the turn, the one who isn't afraid of the object that screeches, a knowledge one doesn't know and the one who in fact has a know-how with it, and, last, the idea of being made a thing. If being made a thing had its previous echoes in the idea of sacrifice, it is now this thing in the hands of my friend that epitomizes for me the feminine as the opening onto desire, the possible elevation of the object. He is of course, for me, the psychoanalyst. In Lacan's theory of discourse there is the quarter turn between the hysteric and the analyst, and I don't think it is possible without a deep love and respect for the unconscious. We are made for that even if we don't know it, or further still, precisely because we don't.

To conclude, Celan, the poet to whom I constantly turn to in order to rehabilitate my relationship to language, to arouse again some obscure piece of desire, comes close to this in his name for poetry. A breathturn, *Atemwende,* he called it. He says, "it is no longer a word. It is a terrifying silence. It takes his and our breath and words away. Poetry is perhaps this: an *Atemwende*, a turning of our breath … It is perhaps here, in this one brief moment, that Medusa's head shrivels and the automatons run down? Perhaps, along with the I, estranged and freed here in this manner, some other thing is also set free?" (Celan, 2005, p. 162). Perhaps. For the life of psychoanalysis, I offer this silence, that freedom. As for me, it's beyond me, but I'm happy.

REFERENCES

Adorno, T. W. (1973). *Negative Dialectics* (E. B. Ashton, trans.). New York: The Seabury Press (original work published in 1966).

Adorno, T. W. (1974). *Minima Moralia: Reflections from Damaged Life* (E. F. N. Jephcott, trans.). London: Verso (original work published in 1951).

Adorno, T. W. (1993). *Hegel: Three Studies* (Shierry Weber Nicholsen, trans.). Boston: MIT Press (original work published in 1963).

Adorno, T. W. (1997). *Aesthetic Theory* (Robert Hullot-Kentor, trans.). Minneapolis: University of Minnesota Press (original work published in 1969).

Adorno, T. W. (2000). *Problems of Moral Philosophy* (Rodney Livingstone, trans.). Stanford: Stanford University Press (original work published in 1996).

Anderson, H. C. (1992). *Hans Anderson's Fairytales: A Selection* (L. W. Kingsland, trans.). Oxford: Oxford University Press (original work published in 1832).

Badiou, A. (1999). *Manifesto for Philosophy* (Norman Madarasz, trans.). Albany, NY: SUNY (original work published in 1989).

Badiou, A. (2000). What Is Love? In: Renata Salecl (ed.), *Sexuation* (pp. 263–282). Durham: Duke University Press.

Badiou, A. (2002). *Ethics: An Essay on the Understanding of Evil* (Peter Hallward, trans.). London: Verso (original work published in 1993).

Badiou, A. (2003a). *On Beckett* (Alberto Toscano, trans.) (Alberto Toscano and Nina Powers, eds.). London: Clinamen Press.

Badiou, A. (2003b). *Saint Paul: The Foundation of Universalism* (Ray Brassier, trans.). Stanford: Stanford University Press (original work published in 1997).

Badiou, A. (2004). *Theoretical Writings* (Ray Brassier, trans.). New York: Continuum.

Badiou, A. (2005a). *Being and Event* (Oliver Feltham, trans.). New York: Continuum (original work published in 1988).

Badiou, A. (2005b). *Handbook of Inaesthetics* (Alberto Toscano, trans.). Stanford: Stanford University Press (original work published in 1998).

Badiou, A. (2005c). *Metapolitics* (Jason Barker, trans.). London: Verso (original work published in 1998).

Badiou, A. (2006a). *Briefings on Existence: A Short Treatise on Transitory Ontology* (Norman Madarasz, trans.). New York: SUNY Press (original work published in 1998).

Badiou, A. (2006b). The Formulas of l'Étourdit (Scott Saviano, trans.). *Lacanian Ink*, 27: 80–96.

Badiou, A. (2008). Philosophy as biography. *The Symptom: Online Journal, 9*, doi: www.lacan.com/symptom9_articles/badiou19.html

Beckett, S. (2006). The Unnameables. In: *The Grove Centenery Edition*, Volume II Novels (pp. 283–408). New York: Grove Press (original work published in 1953).

Binswanger, L. (1957). *Sigmund Freud: Reminiscences of a Friendship.* New York: Grune and Stratton.

Bion, W. (1967). Notes on memory and desire. *The Psychoanalytic Forum*, 2: 271–280.

Britton, R. (1999). Getting in on the act: The hysterical solution. *International Journal of Psychoanalysis*, 80: 1–14.

Cavell, S. (1979). *The Claim of Reason*. Oxford: Oxford University Press.

Celan, P. (2005). *Selected Poems and Prose of Paul Celan* (John Felstiner, trans.) (Pierre Joris, ed.). New York: W. W. Norton.

Clément, C. (1983). *The Lives and Legends of Jacques Lacan* (Arthur Godhammer, trans.). New York: Columbia University Press (original work published in 1981).

Clément, C. (1987). *The Weary Sons of Freud* (Nicole Ball, trans.). London: Verso (original work published in 1978).

Clément, C. & Cixous, H. (1996). *The Newly Born Woman* (Betsy Wing, trans.). London: I. B. Tauris (original work published in 1975).

Clément, C. & Kristeva, J. (2001). *The Feminine and the Sacred* (Jane Marie Todd, trans.). New York: Columbia University Press (original work published in 1998).

Deleuze, G. (1989). *Masochism: Coldness and Cruelty and Venus in Furs* (Jean McNeil and Aude Willm, trans.). New York: Zone Books (original work published in 1967).

Deleuze, G. (1998). *Difference and Repetition* (Paul Patton, trans.). New York: Columbia University Press (original work published in 1968).

Deleuze, G. & Guattari, F. (1983). *Anti-Oedipus: Capitalism and Schitzophrenia* (Robert Hurley, Mark Seem, and Helen R. Lane, trans.). Minneapolis: University of Minnesota Press (original work published in 1972).

Derrida, J. (1978). *Writing and Difference* (Alan Bass, trans.). New York: Routledge.

Derrida, J. (1984). *Of an Apocalyptic Tone Recently Adopted in Philosophy* (J. P. Leavey, trans.). In: *Oxford Literary Review*, 6(no. 2): 3–37.

Derrida, J. (1991). To speculate—on "Freud" (Alan Bass, trans.). In: Peggy Kamuf (Ed.), *A Derrida Reader: Between the Blinds* (pp. 516–168). New York: Columbia University Press.

Derrida, J. (1998). *Resistances of Psychoanalysis* (Peggy Kamuf, et al., trans.) Stanford: Stanford University Press.

Eliot, T. S. (1997). The Sacred Wood: Essays on Poetry and Criticism. London: Faber and Faber (original work published in 1920).

Euripides (2006). *Grief Lessons: Four Plays* (Anne Carson, trans.). New York: New York Review Books.

Fedida, P. (1999). A borderline state of humanity and the fragmented ego of the analyst. In: J. F. Gurewich & M. Tort (eds.), *Lacan and the New Wave in American Psychoanalysis* (pp. 63–73). New York: Other Press.

Freud, S. (1895). *Studies on Hysteria*. S.E. 2. London: Hogarth.

Freud, S. (1899). *Screen Memories*. S.E. 3. London: Hogarth.

Freud, S. (1900). *The Interpretation of Dreams*. S.E. 4, 5. London: Hogarth.

Freud, S. (1905a). *Three Essays on the Theory of Sexuality*. S.E. 7. London: Hogarth.

Freud, S. (1905b). *Fragment of an Analysis of a Case of Hysteria*. S.E. 7. London: Hogarth.

Freud, S. (1910). *A Special Type of Choice of Object made by Men (Contributions to the Psychology of Love, I)*. S.E. 11. London: Hogarth.

Freud, S. (1912). *On the Universal Tendency to Debasement in the Sphere of Love (Contributions to the Psychology of Love II)*. S.E. 11. London: Hogarth.

Freud, S. (1912–1913). *Totem and Taboo*. S.E. 13. London: Hogarth.

Freud, S. (1914). *On Narcissism: An Introduction*. S.E. 14. London: Hogarth.

Freud, S. (1917). *Mourning and Melancholia*. S.E. 14. London: Hogarth.

Freud, S. (1919a). *"A Child is Being Beaten" A Contribution to the Study of the Origin of Sexual Perversions.* S.E. 17. London: Hogarth.

Freud, S. (1919b). *The Uncanny.* S.E. 17. London: Hogarth.

Freud, S. (1921). *Group Psychology and the Analysis of the Ego.* S.E. 18. London: Hogarth.

Freud, S. (1924). *The Dissolution of the Oedipus Complex.* S.E. 19. London: Hogarth.

Freud, S. (1930). *Civilization and its Discontents.* S.E. 21. London: Hogarth.

Freud, S. (1937). *Analysis Terminable and Interminable.* S.E. 23. London: Hogarth.

Freud, S. (1939). *Moses and Monotheism: Three Essays.* S.E. 13. London: Hogarth.

Freud, S. (1985). *The Complete Letters of Sigmund Freud to Wilhelm Fliess 1887–1904* (Jeffrey Moussaieff Masson, trans. and ed.). Massachusettes: Belknap-Harvard Press.

Glover, E. (1931). The therapeutic effect of inexact interpretation: A contribution to the theory of suggestion. *International Journal of Psychoanalysis, 12*: 397–411.

Heidegger, M. (1971). What is a thing? In: *Poetry, Language, Thought* (Albert Hofstadter, trans.) (pp. 161–185). New York: Harper & Row.

Heidegger, M. (1993). *Basic Writings* (David Krell, ed.). San Francisco: Harper Collins.

Irigaray, L. (1985a). *This Sex Which is Not One* (Catherine Porter, trans.). Ithaca: Cornell University Press (original work published in 1977).

Irigaray, L. (1985b). *Speculum of the Other Woman* (Gillian C. Gill, trans.). Ithaca: Cornell University Press (original work published in 1974).

Irigaray, L. (1993). *An Ethics of Sexual Difference* (Carolyn Burke, trans.). Ithaca: Cornell University Press (original work published in 1984).

Johnston, A. (2010). The philosophy which is not one: Jean-Claude Milner, Alain Badiou, and Lacanian anti-philosophy. *S: Journal of the Jan Van Eyck Circle for Lacanian Ideology Critique, 3*: 137–158.

Joyce, J. (1966). *Letters of James Joyce* (Richard Ellman, ed.). New York: Viking.

Joyce, J. (1986). *Ulysses.* New York: Vintage (original work published in 1922).

Kernberg, O. (1967). Borderline personality organization. *Journal of the American Psychoanalytic Association, 15*: 641–685.

Kernberg, O., Seltzer, M., Koenigsberg, J. & Carr, A. (1989). *Psychodynamic Psychotherapy of Borderline Patients.* New York: Basic Books.

Kristeva, J. (1982). *Powers of Horror: An Essay on Abjection* (Leon S. Roudiez, trans.). New York: Columbia University Press (original work published in 1980).

Kristeva, J. (1987). *Tales of Love* (Leon S. Roudiez, trans.). New York: Columbia University Press (original work published in 1983).

Kristeva, J. (1989). *Black Sun: Depression and Melancholia* (Leon S. Roudiez, trans.). New York: Columbia University Press (original work published in 1987).

Lacan, J. (1958). *The Seminar of Jacques Lacan Book VI: Desire and Its Interpretation 1958–1959* (Cormac Gallagher, trans.). Unpublished copy for personal use only.

Lacan, J. (1967). *The Seminar of Jacques Lacan Book XV: The Psychoanalytic Act 1967–1968* (Cormac Gallagher, trans.). Unpublished copy for personal use only.

Lacan, J. (1971a). *The Seminar of Jacques Lacan Book XVIII: On a Discourse That Might Not Be A Semblance* (Cormac Gallagher, trans.). Unpublished copy for personal use only.

Lacan, J. (1971b). *The Seminar of Jacques Lacan Book XIX: ... Ou Pire ... Or Worse* (Cormac Gallagher, trans.). Unpublished copy for personal use only.

Lacan, J. (1973). *The Seminar of Jacques Lacan Book XXI: The Non-Dupes Err 1973–1974* (Cormac Gallagher, trans.). Unpublished copy for personal use only.

Lacan, J. (1975). *The Seminar of Jacques Lacan Book XXIII: The Sinthome 1975–1976* (Cormac Gallagher, trans.). Unpublished copy for personal use only.

Lacan, J. (1981). *The Seminar of Jacques Lacan Book XI: The Four Fundamental Concepts of Psychoanalysis* (Alan Sheridan, trans.). New York: W. W. Norton and Co. (original work published in 1973).

Lacan, J. (1990). *Television* (Denis Hollier, Rosalind Krauss, and Anetter Michelson, trans.) (Joan Copjec, ed.). New York: W. W. Norton and Co. (original work published in 1974).

Lacan, J. (1992). *The Seminar of Jacques Lacan Book VII: The Ethics of Psychoanalysis 1959–1960* (Dennis Porter, trans.). New York: W. W. Norton and Co. (original work published in 1986).

Lacan, J. (1998). *The Seminar of Jacques Lacan Book XX: Encore- On Feminine Sexuality, The Limits of Love and Knowledge, 1972–1973* (Bruce Fink, trans.). New York: W. W. Norton and Co. (original work published in 1975).

Lacan, J. (2001). *Autre écrits*. Paris: Seuil.

Lacan, J. (2006). *Écrits* (Bruce Fink, trans.). New York: W. W. Norton and Co. (original work published in 1970).

Lacan, J. (2007). *The Seminar of Jacques Lacan Book XVII: The Other Side of Psychoanalysis* (Russell Grigg, trans.). New York: W. W. Norton and Co. (original work published in 1991).

Lacan, J., Miller, J.A. & Hulbert, J. (1977) Desire and the Interpretation of Desire in Hamlet. *Yale French Studies*, 55/56: 11–52.

Laplanche, J. (1976). *Life and Death in Psychoanalysis* (Jeffrey Mehlman, trans.). Baltimore: Johns Hopkins University Press (original work published in 1970).

Laplanche, J. (1999). *Essays on Otherness* (John Fletcher, ed.). New York: Routledge.

Leclaire, S. (1998b). *Psychoanalyzing: On the Order of the Unconscious and the Practice of the Letter* (Peggy Kamuf, trans.). Stanford: Stanford University Press (original work published in 1968).

Loraux, N. (1987). *Tragic Ways of Killing a Woman* (Anthony Forster, trans.). Cambridge: Harvard University Press (original work published in 1985).

Loraux, N. (1995). *The Experience of Tiresias: The Feminine and The Greek Man* (Paula Wissing, trans.). Princeton: Princeton University Press.

Loraux, N. (1998). *Mothers in Mourning* (Corinne Pache, trans.). Ithaca: Cornell University Press (original work published in 1988).

Loraux, N. (2006). *The Invention of Athens: The Funeral Oration in the Classical City* (Alan Sheridan, trans.). New York: Zone Books (original work published in 1981).

Miele, P. (2011). Tale telling and the open. *Division/Review*, 1: 37.

Milner, J.-C. (1995). *L'Œuvre Claire: Lacan, la science, la philosophie*. Paris: Seuil.

Montrelay, M. (1977). *L'Ombre Et Le Nom: Sur La Feminite*. Paris: Editions de Minuit.

Montrelay, M. (1984). On folding and unfolding: An example of dream interpretation in analysis. *Psychoanalytic Inquiry*, 4: 193–219.

Pine, F. (2001). Listening and speaking psychoanalytically—With what in mind? *International Journal of Psychoanalysis*, 82: 901–916.

Rapaport, D. (1967). *Collected Papers of David Rapaport*. New York: Basic Books.

Rieff, P. (1959). *Freud: The Mind of the Moralist*. Chicago: University of Chicago.

Roustang, F. (1982). *Dire Mastery: Discipleship from Freud to Lacan* (Ned Lukacher, trans.). Washington DC: American Psychiatric Press (original work published in 1976).

Safouan, M. (1980). In praise of hysteria. In: Stuart Schneiderman (ed.), *Returning to Freud: Clinical Psychoanalysis in the School of Lacan* (pp. 55–61). New Haven: Yale University Press.

Safouan, M. (2003). *Speech or Death? Language as Social Order*. (Martin Thom, trans.). New York: Palgrave Macmillan. (original work published in 1993).

Shakespeare, W. (2003). *Hamlet* (Burton Raffel, Ed.) New Haven: Yale University Press.

Sophocles (1984). *The Three Theban Plays: Antigone, Oedipus the King, Oedipus at Colonus* (Robert Fagles, trans.). New York: Penguin Books.

Verhaeghe, P. (1999). *Does the Woman Exist? From Freud's Hysteric to Lacan's Feminine.* New York: Other Press.

Weil, S. (1952). *Gravity and Grace* (Emma Crawford and Mario von der Ruhr, trans.). London and New York: Routledge (original work published in 1947).

Winnicott, D. W. (1971). *Playing and Reality.* New York: Routledge.

Žižek, S. (1997). *The Plague of Fantasies.* London: Verso.

Žižek, S. (1999). *The Ticklish Subject.* London: Verso.

INDEX